STRESS MANAGEMENT

D0662596

STRESS
MANAGEMENT

VERA PEIFFER

Thorsons
An Imprint of HarperCollins*Publishers*

Thorsons
An Imprint of HarperCollins*Publishers*
77–85 Fulham Palace Road,
Hammersmith, London W6 8JB
1160 Battery Street,
San Francisco, California 94111–1213

Published by Thorsons 1996

10 9 8 7 6 5 4 3 2

© Vera Peiffer 1996

Vera Peiffer asserts the moral right to
be identified as the author of this work

A catalogue record for this book
is available from the British Library

ISBN 0 7225 3243 1

Printed in Great Britain by
Caledonian International Book Manufacturing Ltd, Glasgow

All rights reserved. No part of this publication may be
reproduced, stored in a retrieval system, or transmitted,
in any form or by any means, electronic, mechanical,
photocopying, recording or otherwise, without the prior
permission of the publishers.

FOR MY FRIENDS GEORGES AND LYN

CONTENTS

ACKNOWLEDGEMENTS

The publishers would like to thank Jillie Collings for her suggestion for the title of this series, *Principles of ...*

INTRODUCTION

Anyone who has ever had to struggle through a prolonged period of work overload, be it at home or out in the workplace, will know what it feels like to be physically exhausted and mentally overwrought. Whereas you are perfectly capable of dealing competently with life's ups and downs when you are unstressed, any hiccups in the daily routine become an emotional crisis once the pressure exceeds a certain threshold.

It is an unpleasant experience to feel out of control and unable to stop yourself from overreacting. You watch yourself shouting at the kids or soldiering on at work even though you are too tired to think straight, seemingly unable to stop yourself.

Stress and all its unpleasant side-effects can arise from a great many different factors; work overload is just one of them. Other life events which can put you under pressure are changes in your circumstances, for example if a family member gets seriously ill or if you unexpectedly suffer financial difficulties. As a rule of thumb you could say that any event that significantly changes your daily routine is a *potential* trigger for stress. I say 'potential' because a lot will depend on your general attitude to change. Stress is not just generated by circumstances; your attitude *towards* the circumstances will have a significant impact on how you cope.

This book looks at a variety of potential stress-triggers. You may be surprised to learn that even events which we would generally label 'positive', such as a promotion or a holiday, can create stress! You will also learn how to deal with difficult situations in a more constructive way, on not just a practical but also an emotional level. You may not be able to cut out all challenges from your life – nor may you want to – but you can certainly do a lot to eliminate unnecessary stresses. You have a lot more power inside you than you might think; *Principles of Stress Management* shows you how to access this power and how to make use of it. In addition, this book provides you with questionnaires for self-assessment and mental exercises which will help you take control of your life, as well as useful information and tips on foods, physical exercise and supplements which can strengthen your resilience to stress. Why be harassed if you can be composed? Why fight if you can play? You may not be able to see a way out of your situation, but it is there before you.

As you read through this book you will quickly find the chapters that are relevant to your particular circumstances, as well as the solutions that suit you best. You will find that you can rid yourself of unnecessary stress and heighten your general sense of well-being at the same time, so that you feel more energetic, more in control, better about yourself and better within yourself. Why not put some of the suggestions in this book into practice? You have nothing to lose but stress!

PART 1

STRESS – HOW IT HAPPENS

I n this first section we will look in detail at what constitutes 'stress', as we commonly call the experience of negative pressure. As your personality plays a part in how you deal with stress, this section includes descriptions of various personality types (their strengths and weaknesses, etc.), followed by a questionnaire (*see Chapter 3*) which will allow you to assess which type you come closest to. Learning about yourself allows you not only to take better care of yourself but also to make positive changes more easily. The better you understand what makes you tick, the greater the control you have over changing your life for the better.

In Chapter 4 we will examine the most common external stressors that may play a part in the build-up to stress, both in work and private life. Depending on your personal beliefs and attitudes, you will deal with these outside stressors more or less effectively. People respond to difficult situations according to their past experiences by using, either consciously or subconsciously, coping strategies which they have acquired over the years. How you cope with stress will also depend on how much external support you get while you are in the difficult situation. All these factors – personality, beliefs, past experiences and external support – work together to shape your physical and emotional reactions to stress, which ultimately determine how much you are affected by a difficulty and how well you deal with it.

WHAT STRESS IS
AND WHAT IT IS NOT

Generally speaking, stress can be caused by our need to adapt physically, mentally and emotionally to a change. This, of course, does not have to be a negative process. If you have finally achieved a promotion which you have worked towards over a long period of time, this is likely to be a very pleasant change which fills you with excitement and satisfaction. However, if you have been persuaded by your superiors to go for the promotion when you do not really feel ready for it, you can end up feeling very nervous and unconfident when this change takes place.

A small amount of stress is useful; it adds interest and motivation to life and keeps us on our toes. Changes that we perceive as moderate are not just harmless but also invigorating, as our adaptability needs to be trained regularly to stay in working order. As we practise going with the flow and dealing with changes, we become stronger. However, when the changes become too great or when they influence our lives negatively over a period of time, our capacity to adapt can become overstretched.

We all have a need to maintain physical and emotional equilibrium. It is when we are on an even keel that we feel comfortable and happy. Any change, especially an unpleasant one,

4   threatens our equilibrium. In order to redress the balance we react with a stereotyped reaction which Hans Selye in his book *The Stress of Life* identified as the General Adaptation Syndrome (GAS). This syndrome springs into action as soon as a person perceives or experiences a stressor. First, the mind goes through the *alarm stage* where the body switches into overdrive. The muscles tense, adrenalin pumps through the system, blood-pressure rises. During the second stage, the *resistance stage*, all the heightened physical and mental responses help create increased activity so that the challenge can be met, but there is only so much strength and endurance that a person can muster before he or she goes to the third stage: *exhaustion*.

As you can imagine, if your capacity to adapt to change is in overdrive for too long, it can make you ill. If you have to cope day-in, day-out with a difficult and demanding boss who only criticizes but never praises, it will eventually wear you down. If you are looking after a bedridden relative all by yourself without getting any help or support, you can easily develop a physical or mental illness yourself. In extreme cases, prolonged exposure to stress can lead to physical and/or emotional breakdown.

By the time someone reaches the third stage it will be obvious that there is a problem. It is easier, however, to ignore the signs of the first two stages. Even though the term 'alarm stage' seems to indicate that you become consciously aware that a change is imminent, this is not necessarily so. At the alarm stage your body and mind get ready for action, but as this preparation happens unconsciously and therefore automatically, it can easily be overlooked. (In Part II of this book you will have an opportunity to check which physical, mental, emotional and behavioural signs you might experience while you are in the resistance stage, or even in the alarm stage – *see page 40*.)

You will already have noticed that stress is not a clear-cut matter which can be defined in objective terms. You may find that the best way of describing stress is at a totally subjective level, as any change that makes you feel uncomfortable physically or emotionally. This definition allows for individual differences in attitude and perception towards stressors.

A subjective definition also makes clear that stress is not the same thing as a great workload, a lot of responsibility or having demands made on you. If these scenarios were automatically synonymous with stress, then *nobody* could be expected to experience them free of stress. However, there are people who have a lot to do and yet stay unstressed by it; there are people who carry great responsibility and who cope with it very well. Stress is only partly a result of the situation itself; it is also, to an extent, caused by our attitude towards that situation. This explains why different people react differently to stress. Look around you while you sit on a commuter train when it is stuck between stations. Some people are simply bored, others annoyed, still others anxious.

Physiologically, the same thing happens to all of us when stress sets in. As soon as we perceive a situation as potentially threatening, our primitive stress response of 'fight or flight' springs into action. Our breathing rate increases (thereby providing the brain and the muscles with more oxygen), the heart rate increases, blood-pressure rises, sugars and fats are released into the bloodstream for extra energy, muscles tense up, the flow of saliva decreases and perspiration increases. All our senses are on 'red alert', and adrenalin and cortisol are released which mobilize the body. These spontaneous physical reactions are very useful when your house in on fire because they enable you to run faster and get away from danger more quickly. However, when you have the same automatic reactions when you are only thinking about tomorrow's meeting at work, you are in trouble. Whereas in the first instance all that extra physical energy and tension are put to good use, in the second

PRINCIPLES OF STRESS MANAGEMENT

example this excess energy has nowhere to go – as you sit there worrying about the next day's meeting, your stress hormones go round and round in your system, keeping everything buzzing in overdrive. For some people this means an increase in gastric juice secretion, which can ultimately lead to ulcers if the stress response kicks in on a regular basis. Also, the prolonged presence of stress and heavy demands on our ability to adapt can exhaust the body and increase the risk of damaging the function of organs such as the heart or the kidneys.

If you feel that you are particularly prone to unnecessary stress reactions, the next two chapters should help you pinpoint the reasons for this.

SUMMARY

- Stress is evoked by our need to re-establish an equilibrium when changes occur.

- Small amounts of stress are necessary and beneficial.

- The three stress stages are alarm, resistance and exhaustion.

- Certain personality types are more prone to stress than others.

- Prolonged stress can lead to illness or mental breakdown.

- The body reacts to stress by mobilizing physical responses to help us cope better with situations which we perceive as threatening.

- Even our thoughts can create a physical stress response.

ARE YOU A
STRESS-PRONE TYPE?

We perceive changes and stressors in our own unique ways. Depending on our background, upbringing and present circumstances, we may find ourselves coping with stress much better than our neighbour or colleague at work. Some of us are born with greater resilience than others, enabling us to stay calm longer than the next person when the going gets tough.

Apart from resilience and adaptability to change, we also bring with us particular dispositions when we are born. Anyone who has children or who is close to a family with small children will be able to confirm how different they are right from the start. One baby is placid and sleeps through the night very early on, whereas another baby will be more wakeful and excitable. One child plays happily on his own, whereas another one has to be entertained a lot to be content. These individual predispositions, together with the manner in which parents bring up their children, will result in various personality types – some of which are particularly vulnerable to stress.

THE ANXIOUS TYPE

This personality type will be lacking somewhat in self-confidence, unsure of his or her abilities even if others try to be reassuring. Anxious people are reluctant to express any negative emotions openly and are often incapable of saying 'no' if someone makes unreasonable demands on them. This unwillingness and fear to stand up for themselves comes either from a distorted sense of duty (something that has usually been drummed into them during childhoood) or from the mistaken belief that they will make themselves unpopular if they do not comply with other people's wishes. Even though anxious people appear to be conformist, they often harbour strong resentments against those whose wishes they seem to carry out so willingly.

STRESS PROBLEMS

Anxious people tend to go for undemanding jobs, which can easily lead them to becoming frustrated and bored. If they progress to a more responsible job they tend to feel easily hassled when the workload increases and will often take their unease out on others.

THE PERFECTIONIST

Perfectionists like everything to be in its proper place and done at the proper time. Routine is of great importance, as is detail. Mistakes are not tolerated – they will even rewrite a handwritten, informal message if their pen slips or a word has been misspelled. This rather plodding way of dealing with life works out well as long as the job in hand is stable and predictable. Perfectionists are usually hard-working and reliable, but not equipped to deal with sudden emergencies or change.

Their great problems adapting to change, and their unwillingness to give up established routines, can cause stress for perfectionists if they find themselves distracted from their routines. Their diligent attention to detail means that they are creating stress for themselves when better prioritization and a more even-handed approach to less important tasks could easily save the day.

THE STIMULUS-SEEKER

This personality type strives on risk and is often addicted to the rush of adrenalin which accompanies any venture. Stimulus-seekers have a certain dare-devil attitude and can be quite brilliant at what they are doing, be it in sports or in the business world. However, they have a very limited attention span. Once the thrill is over, they move on to the next project. They are often not concerned with details and leave others to do the menial parts of a job while they attend to the 'big picture'. Stimulus-seekers will typically choose professions where risk-taking promises to yield great amounts of money and/or esteem.

STRESS PROBLEMS

Stimulus-seekers experience the risks of their ventures as beneficial stress, and thrive on it. Their minds race with possibilities rather than worries, and as a consequence they tend to smoke and drink too much. Substance abuse and its negative side-effects are more common in stimulus-seekers than are mental and/or physical illness.

THE AMBITIOUS TYPE (A-TYPE)

A-type personalities tend to be hard-driven and aggressive, channelling all their energies into their work. A-types have little or no time for a social life or hobbies; they live, think and dream 'work'. They have problems delegating and are highly critical of themselves and others, often becoming impatient and angry when things do not run smoothly. They find it impossible to sit down quietly and do nothing; they are constantly moving, jiggling their knees and tapping their fingers – in times of stress they tend to do several things at the same time. They also find it hard to concentrate fully on conversations because they are already racing ahead in their mind, thinking about the next thing they want to do.

The A-type personality is the stress category that has been most widely studied. This type is found not just in high-level jobs, but all the way through the various strata of society.

STRESS PROBLEMS

In their efforts to control everything and everyone around them, A-types exert themselves physically and mentally. They are unable to recognize when they have reached their limit and will typically suffer from high blood-pressure. A-types are prone to coronary heart disease, ulcers and atherosclerosis (hardening of the arteries).

All stress-prone types of personality are driven by one thing: fear. The anxious person is afraid to be unpopular and to be considered unhelpful; the perfectionist is afraid of being 'only human'; the stimulus-seeker is afraid of boredom; and the A-type is afraid of not being seen to achieve. Even though certain personality traits can predispose a person to have these fears, one's upbringing also plays a part. Below we look at some of the factors that can lead to a personality type that is vulnerable to stress.

PRESSURE TO SUCCEED

When children are pressurized by parents and teachers constantly to achieve the very best results, and if love and approval are dependent on high performance, some children will internalize these conditions and later live their lives accordingly. Self-worth becomes totally dependent on achievements. Without achievements, they feel that they are nobody and that nobody will respect them. Within these rules there is no room for grey areas; there is only black and white.

CRITICISM

When criticized frequently and in an unconstructive manner, some children will withdraw, hoping to avoid further humiliation by keeping a low profile. They stop trying out new things, become anxious and unconfident in their own abilities and grow up to live their lives trying to please others and gain their approval in an attempt to maintain their own self-esteem.

LONELINESS

When children are shown little or no affection or interest they can grow up without self-worth or confidence in their own validity as human beings. As a consequence, their entry into the adult world of work can constitute an escape from these feelings of worthlessness. In their attempt to justify their existence, they may dedicate themselves over-zealously to their work.

OVERPROTECTION

Parents who do everything for their children prevent them from becoming independent and from having the opportunity to test their strength against the everyday world. This restrictive upbringing can lead to resentment and rebellion, coupled with great fear at what there is 'out there'. As overprotected children grow up they keep on struggling with the same issues – not wanting to be controlled but at the same time fearing the freedom of being an independent person.

Now that we have looked at the personality types most affected negatively by stress, and some of the factors leading to becoming one of these types, it is time for you to judge for yourself whether you are in fact more prone to stress than most.

QUESTIONNAIRE: CHECK YOUR PERSONALITY STRESS FACTORS

This questionnaire is made up of four categories of questions, grouped together according to the stress types we looked at in the previous chapter. Make a note of each statement that is true for you, giving yourself 1 point for each. Try to do this quickly, without pondering over individual statements for too long.

WHAT ANXIOUS PEOPLE SAY ABOUT THEMSELVES

- Others take advantage of me but I feel unable to stop them.

- I am very upset by rows, even if they are between other people.

- I prefer the devil I know rather than change to something new, even if it could be better for me.

- I find it difficult to express my needs to others because I feel this might be selfish and self-indulgent.

- Even if the other person has made a mistake, it is me who ends up apologizing.

- I find it very difficult to take the initiative, either socially or professionally.

- I cannot openly show my emotions, especially not the negative ones like anger or annoyance.

- I never seem to get what I want.

WHAT PERFECTIONISTS SAY ABOUT THEMSELVES

- I need to have everything 'just so'.

- I plan and carry out any work I do to the highest possible standard.

- I greatly dislike it when my daily routine gets disrupted.

- I am upset when things are not done as they should be done.

- I get very agitated when I am prevented from finishing a job properly; I can only relax when all the 't's are crossed and 'i's dotted.

- My thoroughness makes me fall behind quite often.

- I find myself mulling over how I could have done things better in the past.

- When I have made only one small mistake, I have to do the whole job again, no matter how trivial the job itself is.

WHAT STIMULUS-SEEKERS SAY
ABOUT THEMSELVES

- I get bored easily.

- The only way you can further yourself is by taking risks.

- I find it difficult to see a task through to the end.

- I cannot be bothered with fiddly details.

- I could never fit into an environment that required me to do routine work.

- I do not like to be tied down in a steady relationship.

- My business ventures take precedence over any private matters.

- I am always thinking up new projects and ventures.

WHAT AMBITIOUS (A-TYPE) PEOPLE
SAY ABOUT THEMSELVES

- I am totally dedicated to any task I undertake.

- I will always make sure I complete anything I start.

- I can focus on my work to the total exclusion of other things.

- I often forget to eat because I am so engrossed in my work.

- I am only happy when I have a full diary.

- I do not have time for a social life unless it is in connection with my work.

- I can never really switch off from work.

• As soon as I have accomplished one task, I start on the next one.

How many points did you get in each section?

If you have four or more points in any one category, you have a strong tendency towards that personality type.

Very few people are a 'classic' specimen of any of the four types, but knowing which of the four you are most similar to can give you a good starting point for understanding what is driving you and how you can make adjustments to reduce your stress levels.

WHAT IS CAUSING YOU STRESS?

As mentioned in Chapter 1, there are of course many different causes of stress, and what is stressful to one person will not be to another. While it is beyond the scope of this book to describe *all* the possible causes of stress, this chapter outlines some of the most common culprits.

Stress is most commonly associated with a heavy workload or with having to shoulder great responsibility; the underlying cause of one's reaction to stress may involve many other factors as well. Both home and the workplace can become the scene of many triggers for physical and mental tension which can gradually build up and, if left unchecked, can develop into a serious health risk.

WORK STRESSORS

The work environment is a veritable breeding ground for stress, for a variety of reasons. Wherever several people get together on a regular basis, tension becomes a possibility. Personalities can clash and roles within a group can be unclear and consequently adversely influence the effectiveness of the group as a whole. Rivalries often develop which lead to wranglings that have nothing to do with the job in hand, and general dissent about aims and procedures can mar the successful completion of an assignment or project.

Time pressure and deadlines are often part of a job, with projects having to be completed by a given date. In theory this should work well, provided everyone involved pulls his or her own weight. Unfortunately, things do not always run smoothly. Deadlines are sometimes set by people not directly involved in a project, which means they may be unreasonably tight, or even impossible to meet. The result? Everyone involved ends up feeling frustrated and angry.

Unless you work for yourself, most people have to report to someone in a higher position, and a lot of stress can arise if the boss is not a good leader or communicator. People are often promoted to leadership positions only on the strength of their professional skill and knowledge. Whereas they may have been excellent members of staff, they may not make very good heads of a department or sector. Very often, an inability to communicate effectively is at the root of the problem.

Then there are the difficult colleagues ... Anyone who has ever worked with or for a difficult person will know how exhausting it can be. If there is friction between people in an office (be it open or implied) anger and resentment can fester, making you stressed out and, eventually, ill.

There are three main types of people who can create upheaval in the workplace – the Bully, who hassles anyone below him or her in the pecking order; the Backstabber, who has an inferiority complex and is nice to your face and puts you down when you have left the room; and the Shirker, who disappears whenever the going gets tough, leaving everyone else to sort out the problem. (We shall look at these three in more detail in Chapter 14.)

Unfortunately, women in particular are still often at the receiving end of bullying and harassment. Even though things have improved over the last few decades, woman are still not treated as equals in many work environments. Certain professions will only reluctantly allow women into their top ranks and, if they do, women still have to work doubly hard and are often paid less than their male counterparts. For the female employee, all this strain is often in addition to the responsibility of having to look after her family when she gets home in the evenings ...

Stress can also evolve directly from your working environment. If you have to work with inadequate equipment this can affect you just as greatly as having to do a day's typing on an uncomfortable chair that makes your back hurt so much you cannot concentrate after a while. Physical stressors can also include bad lighting, poor ventilation, and pollutants (such as cigarette smoke) in the air. An unpleasant or unsuitable environment can cause you not only to feel ill, but does little to boost morale among the members of the workforce who have to put up with it.

Then of course there is the situation of working on your own. It is a fairly modern phenomenon for people to run their own businesses from home or from modest office premises. It takes a dedicated and disciplined person to make working alone a success. You need to be highly motivated and have a strong sense of direction to get through the times when job-related matters do not progress as well as you would like them to, and when there is no one there to discuss things with you can easily end up feeling lonely and isolated.

DOMESTIC STRESSORS

As mentioned regarding work stressors, wherever there are people there is the possibility of stress. Just because at home the people around you are related to you does not mean that there are no power struggles going on!

An obvious cause of stress is disagreement or tension among family members. This can arise from a basic incompatibility between partners. When children are involved, an untenable marriage is often kept going in the belief that this will be better for the children. In reality, children suffer just as much, if not more, by living in a strained atmosphere at home than if they lived with one relatively happy parent.

Any instability in family life, be it rows or frequent absences of one partner, causes stress. Maybe one parent is away from home a lot because of business or the nature of his or her job, leaving the other to cope. Any decisions concerning the children have to be made by this parent, and in addition he or she has to shoulder all the responsibility if things do not work out and the children get into difficulties. With bullying, truancy and racism rife at many schools, and with the increased availability of drugs even in rural areas, it can be incredibly difficult – and stressful – bringing up children today.

If it is stressful to have healthy children, it is even more so when you have a child who is disabled or severely ill. Special children need help to do things which other youngsters can do unaided, and as there are only 24 hours in a day, loving parents will often end up neglecting themselves in the process. This can cause serious health problems for the parents, the stresses manifesting themselves both physically and mentally.

Of course, actual crises such as seeing your child or anyone else close to you die of an incurable disease or losing a baby through cot death are among the most tragic life situations you can be faced with.

But it is not just one's immediate family who can be the cause of stress. What happens if your parents are no longer able to look after themselves, when they become too frail or unwell to run their own household? Some very difficult decisions have to be made, and these decisions are not only dependent on personalities but also on finances and circumstances. Considerable change is brought about by having one or two extra people in the house, people who have their own ways of doing things, their own habits and routines. This situation is not only stressful for the children, but also for the ageing parents who are trying to adapt to their new environment.

Today we understand that stress symptoms can also emerge when a family member has difficulties getting past a particular stage in the life cycle, such as becoming an adult, moving in with or marrying someone, becoming a parent, seeing the children leave home, and retirement. Each of these stages brings its own difficulties; people may find themselves having to adjust to their new role in life even as they work through letting go of the old one.

OTHER STRESSORS

Any changes that disrupt your daily routine are stressful to a greater or lesser extent, depending on your general disposition and circumstances. When you lose your job or find yourself in financial trouble for any other reason, this will cause great worry and concern – money problems have a direct knock-on effect on so many other matters in life.

Interestingly, even what we would consider to be *positive* changes can create stress, such as holidays or a promotion. The reason is that when you are taken out of your familiar home or work environment, you will automatically have to adjust to your new situation, and this involves the expenditure of extra mental energy, often coupled with a sense of anxiety.

Your immediate environment also has a great influence on your well-being. If you live in an isolated area (whether in a rural backwater or an anonymous block of flats), stress can be brought about by the fact that you have too little personal contact with other people.

Also, in areas where crime or violence are common, just leaving the house can be very stressful. Equally distressing are neighbours with antisocial habits who quarrel loudly or play their music at top volume in the middle of the night, just as any other form of noise pollution (say from nearby airports or factories) can disturb your sense of equilibrium and, therefore, invoke a stress reaction.

PART 2

WHAT HAPPENS WHEN YOU FALL INTO THE STRESS TRAP ...

I t is important to understand the warning signals that your body and mind send out in response to a physical or emotional overload. By acquainting yourself with these stress symptoms you will be able to recognize and deal with them quickly and effectively, before they get out of hand.

There are some warning signs that people readily associate with stress, such as excessive smoking, tiredness, headaches and irritability. But did you know that the habit of checking and re-checking whether you have locked your front door or turned off the cooker is also a symptom caused by stress? Or were you aware that a bad memory can be a sign of stress?

Understanding which form stress can take also gives you a better choice of how to combat it. You may decide that, rather than popping a pill when a tension headache crops up you will learn to relax more fully (*page 64*); that rather than taking sedatives for anxiety you will deal with what is causing the anxiety in the first place – this might involve becoming more assertive and being able to state your own needs more clearly (*page 87*).

PHYSICAL REACTIONS

O ur internal organs are controlled and regulated, without our conscious effort, by the autonomic (or vegetative) nervous system (ANS). The ANS consists of two antagonistic sets of nerves, the *sympathetic* and the *parasympathetic* nervous systems. The former connects the internal organs to the brain by spinal nerves; it prepares the organism for fight or flight when stress occurs. The nerve fibres of the parasympathetic nervous system, on the other hand, consist of cranial nerves and lumbar spinal nerves and have the task of getting the body back to normal after it has been aroused by the sympathetic nervous system.

This means that the sympathetic nervous system, once it is aroused, will set in motion a number of physical processes such as general muscle tension, dilation of the pupils, restriction of the flow of saliva in the mouth, dilation of the bronchi, opening of the pores and increased perspiration, constriction of the bowels and loosening of the bladder. In addition, the liver is activated to release sugar into the blood to produce extra energy, and hormones such as adrenalin and corticosteroids are pumped out into the system, accelerating breathing and increasing the heart rate. While all this is going on the autonomic nervous system slows down digestion processes.

Once the stress-inducing situation is over, the parasympathetic branch of the nervous system reverses all the above processes – the pupils contract again, saliva starts flowing freely once more, the bronchi contract, the heart rate slows down, the pores close, the bladder contracts and digestion is stimulated, as is the release of bile which helps digest fats.

To help you understand these physical processes we will take a look at a typical situation that produces some common stress symptoms.

SITUATION

You are worried about having to give a talk in front of a group of people. As you prepare for it, you become aware of the following physical reactions in yourself:

- your mouth goes dry and your voice becomes more high-pitched (flow of saliva restricted, muscles in throat tense)
- your heart beats faster and your breathing becomes irregular (chest muscles tense up and bronchi dilate, adrenalin is released)
- you need to go to the toilet to pass water more often than usual (bladder loosened)
- you are constipated or have stomach cramps (muscles tense up)
- your hands feel clammy (pores open and perspiration increases)
- you feel anxious and have 'butterflies' in your stomach (adrenalin is pumping through your system)
- you feel restless and pace up and down, your hands shaking and your knees trembling (blood sugar levels are up to provide more energy; adrenalin and corticosteroids accelerate body processes).

As you can see, these physical symptoms are not all in the mind but are caused by very real changes in your blood chemistry, activated by the sympathetic nervous system. However, it is your mind that ultimately determines how strongly your body reacts to change or unusual circumstances. Depending on your attitudes, beliefs and general predisposition you will assess a situation as either harmless or dangerous. Some people positively thrive on challenges and are at their best when they need to deal with unforeseen situations; others will feel threatened and stressed.

The effects of the sympathetic nervous system can be very beneficial, provided they do not come into play too often or too excessively. A slight increase in body tension, together with higher energy levels and the associated faster reaction time, is of great value if you have to perform well; it is when these reactions become excessive that problems result and we are less likely to cope well.

When the sympathetic nervous system is stimulated repeatedly and over a long period of time, your body may be able to adapt for a while, but as soon as any additional demands are made on it – such as those brought about by an unhealthy diet, smoking, drinking or lack of sleep – your system gets overloaded and can break down. Being in physical overdrive can become a habit, and if there is never a chance for the parasympathetic nervous system to kick into gear and reverse the process, you wear down your inner organs. This is analogous to driving your car at high speed in a low gear all the time – eventually you have problems with the engine.

Even though both the sympathetic and parasympathetic nervous systems are functioning on an involuntary level, we can activate the parasympathetic system by setting some time aside each day to relax properly – and this is *not* the same thing as putting up your feet and lighting a cigarette! Adapting your diet so that it contains more easily digestible foods also helps

28 (*see page 111*), as does working on becoming more confident (*see page 92*) and developing a more positive outlook (*see page 101*).

WARNING SIGNS

PHYSICAL STRESS SYMPTOMS

- tension (in the throat, chest, stomach, shoulders, neck, jaws)
- headache and migraine
- backache
- neck ache
- irregular breathing
- palpitations
- breathlessness even when at rest
- restlessness and fidgeting
- tics (face, eyes, mouth, etc.)
- dry mouth
- high-pitched voice
- sweating
- cold hands and feet
- shakiness
- dizziness
- exhaustion
- stomach ache and 'butterflies' in stomach
- indigestion
- nausea
- increased need to urinate
- diarrhoea
- sleeping problems
- sexual problems
- ulcers
- increased sensitivity to noise

CASE HISTORY: PALPITATIONS

(All names used in this and the other Case Histories in this book have been changed to ensure confidentiality.)
Gary (42) was running his own business and was doing well financially, but all was not well at home. He had recently married; his wife Jenny had two teenage children from a previous marriage. Even though Gary was fond of the children he was not getting on with them as well as he had hoped. Arguments erupted frequently, not only between Gary and the children but also between Gary and Jenny. Gary felt that Jenny was spoiling the children by being too lenient with them, whereas Jenny accused Gary of being jealous of her affection for them.

After six months of rows and arguments Gary began to notice that every time he sat down to rest or go to sleep his heart would start racing. When these palpitations became more frequent he started to worry that there might be something wrong with his heart, but after a thorough check-up his doctor assured Gary that his heart was perfectly all right and that the symptoms were stress-related.

Gary decided that, rather than take beta blockers or sedatives, he was going to try to work through his problems with Jenny. Together they visited a marriage guidance counsellor, who helped them develop a workable, co-operative strategy for dealing with the children. Gary also took a few lessons in relaxation to bring his stress level down. After six weeks his palpitations had decreased considerably; after a further four weeks they had disappeared altogether.

(More about the methods Gary used can be found on *page 64* [relaxation] and *page 92* [addressing problems].)

MENTAL AND
EMOTIONAL REACTIONS

The interdependence between body and mind, as described in the previous section, means that physical stress symptoms will affect your mental efficiency and emotional balance. Depending on how severely you experience stress, your mental and emotional symptoms will be more or less pronounced. Typical mental reactions include racing thoughts and difficulty concentrating – as if your mind has gone into overdrive and is unable to slow down. This is why it is often impossible to go to sleep when you are stressed; your overactive mind will not let you! Apart from causing insomnia, this kind of muddled thinking and lack of concentration also leads to memory problems and difficulty retaining new information. Efficient recall depends on a focused and calm mind. If your mind is frantic no information will go into your memory and nothing can be retrieved from it, as anyone who has ever suffered from exam nerves will know.

Because you have problems concentrating when you are under stress, you are more likely to make mistakes. Your judgement is impaired and you may make rash decisions, just to get a problem out of the way. Again this can cause you to make mistakes, which in turn can dent your confidence. Some people find that rather than make irrational decisions they shy away from decision-making altogether when they are under stress. They feel harassed by life and everyone around them, and want nothing more than to be left alone. Responsibilities that were once perfectly acceptable suddenly become burdensome.

The main effect of a stressed mind is that you lose your perspective. As your brain is racing ahead and you try in vain to keep up with it, you lose your balanced frame of reference. You have difficulties prioritizing sensibly, you feel unduly rushed – even when no one is rushing you – and you become disorganized. A certain symptom of stress is when you start lots of jobs but do not finish any of them.

The curious thing about mental overdrive is that it can be quite addictive for some. Whether you like hyperactive brain activity or not, you may be reluctant to let go of it. Just like the stuntman who gets a buzz from facing dangerous situations again and again, so some people thrive on the rush of adrenalin that comes with tight deadlines, difficult business deals and tough negotiations. Even those who do not enjoy mental overdrive often find it hard to stop thinking and worrying excessively. This may be partly due to their lack of understanding about how to stop, but they may also suffer from the almost superstitious belief that, unless they worry and fret, something is going to go terribly wrong. In this sense they do not really want to relax.

The emotional side-effects of stress which go hand in hand with an overactive mind are usually so unpleasant that the sufferer seeks relief after a while. Among the emotional responses are mood changes, aggression and tearfulness. Even if you are experiencing these emotional symptoms you may not be aware of them because they tend to progress gradually over time. We all have a certain capacity for adapting to stress, and as long as no further stress builds up on top of the original amount we usually cope adequately even though we might find ourselves a bit more short-tempered and cynical than before. These negative changes may not be apparent to us because we are too busy dealing with the issues that are making us feel stressed. It is when the stress will not abate that our impatience and cynicism start to grow, possibly out of proportion. Whereas we were reasonable and had a generally positive outlook before, we have now seemingly changed personality.

The way these emotional changes progress depends on your general predisposition. Some people become dejected, feel depressed and consider themselves a failure; others feel anxious or even panicky and struggle with feelings of guilt about their perceived inadequacy; still others develop phobias or tics or start suffering from nightmares. A distorted perspective often results in an altered perception of yourself and others, and always for the worse. As you feel dejected and incompetent you begin not to like yourself very much and also suspect others of feeling the same. Some people find it difficult to express their feelings about how stress is getting to them; instead they shout, cry or kick the cat ... This usually results in a vicious circle, where their fear of being disliked becomes reality as a result of their behaviour. This, in turn, creates more stress: 'I knew nobody really likes me, and here is the proof!'

WARNING SIGNS

MENTAL STRESS SYMPTOMS

- lack of concentration
- forgetfulness
- inability to remember recent events
- inability to take in new information
- lack of co-ordination
- mind going around in circles
- indecisiveness

- irrational or rash decision-making
- being disorganized
- making mistakes more frequently
- misjudging people and situations
- inaccuracy
- struggling with simple tasks (adding up, working simple machinery)
- paying inordinate attention to detail

EMOTIONAL STRESS SYMPTOMS

- anxiety
- phobias
- panic and panic attacks
- feeling persecuted
- aggression
- cynicism
- guilt
- depression
- mood swings
- tearfulness
- nightmares
- feeling abandoned
- excessive worrying
- loss of sense of humour
- withdrawal

SUCCESSFUL STRESS MANAGEMENT

CASE HISTORY: POOR MEMORY

Linda (37) had been working in her job for five years when her company was hit by recession. A great number of people were made redundant in order to keep the company afloat. Linda felt lucky that she had been kept on, but her workload seemed to double practically overnight. Whereas before she had felt competent and in control, Linda now described herself as struggling to keep her head above water. She was particularly worried by her forgetfulness and inability to remember conversations she had had with colleagues or issues that had been raised in meetings. Her mind seemed to run riot whenever she tried to concentrate, only to go blank when she tried to remember something, even if she'd learned the information quite recently. As a consequence, Linda made a few embarrassing mistakes at work which left her feeling inadequate and also concerned that she might lose her job after all if she did not improve.

Linda decided to seek the help of a hypnotherapist. During her hypnotherapy sessions Linda learned some techniques to help her relax physically and mentally. In order to reinforce the positive effects of these techniques Linda's therapist gave her a self-hypnosis relaxation tape which she played regularly in the evenings before going to bed. This, in conjunction with some positive thinking exercises, enabled her to regain a lot of ground at work. After four sessions Linda reported that her ability to concentrate and her memory had significantly improved; also, her sense of humour had returned.

(Details of the methods Linda used can be found on *page 64* [physical relaxation], *page 69* [mental relaxation] and *page 101* [positive thinking].)

BEHAVIOURAL REACTIONS

S ome people, rather than displaying an overtly emotional reaction to stress, experience negative changes in their behaviour. Some of these changes in behaviour may not appear to be linked to stress at all. Most of us would readily recognize excessive smoking as a stress-related behaviour, but when someone honks his horn and gesticulates wildly while we are sitting in a traffic jam we probably don't immediately think his problem is that he is over-stressed!

Our behaviour and reactions are governed by three factors – our personality, our past experiences, and our present circumstances. Our personality will dictate our behavioural *tendencies*. If you are an introvert you are more likely to react to stress by withdrawing rather than by lashing out, as an extro-vert might. A placid personality will have a much higher stress threshold than a 'racehorse' personality whose stress responses are triggered much earlier by more minor events.

Our past experiences will also contribute to our present-day behaviour. Past experiences, especially those in childhood and adolescence help form our attitudes and beliefs, and our expectations for the future. If, for example, we have grown up in a loving and supportive environment where we received help when we had trouble dealing with a situation, we begin to learn how to deal with difficult situations without panicking. This means that we react much less readily to stress later on in life compared to those who have had guilt and shame heaped on them whenever they made a mistake or had problems learning something.

The third component that influences our behaviour and our reactions is our present environment and circumstances. You have already read earlier in this book about the effects of environmental stressors like living in an unsafe neighbourhood or being subjected to noise pollution, for example. Even the most laid-back personality will get worn down eventually by a stereo next door that is turned up to full volume every night. Equally, unexpected financial problems put enormous pressures on all of us. Even in these difficult circumstances, a positive attitude and a constructive approach can be your saving grace. Happily, your attitude is something you can work on (*page 101*) if you have not already developed a positive outlook in your younger years.

Quite a few behavioural reactions to stress are an exaggeration of an existing habit. If you already have a slight tendency to overeat, bite your nails or worry, you will probably find that in times of stress you start bingeing, reducing your nails to half their size or developing obsessive thoughts or compulsive habits. Ex-smokers find that when stress creeps up to a certain level they fall back into the habit of smoking, even though they may not have smoked in a long time.

The behavioural stress reactions that are hardest to understand are obsessions and compulsions. An *obsession* is a persistent idea or thought in your mind which terrifies you, even though you know the thought is totally irrational. Obsessional thoughts come out of the blue and can be something like 'Today I am going to die' or 'Today I will harm my children.' Even though sufferers reject these thoughts, they are unable to stop them. In order to counteract these terrifying ideas the obsessive person will often go through a ritualistic *compulsive* action. This can be, for example, washing your hands every time you have touched anything, having to tap on every doorframe a certain number of times before you enter a room, or checking continually that the ornaments on the mantle-piece are in a particular order. If anyone tries to stop this compulsive action, the sufferer gets extremely agitated and panicky.

A mild form of compulsion is one that many people go through as children – not stepping on cracks in the pavement. These mild forms are usually called superstitions and are fairly harmless. However, when a habit or a thought begins to disrupt everyday life, the problem obviously needs professional attention.

People who develop obsessions and compulsions tend to be highly critical of themselves and others, have a strong perfectionist streak and are over-conscientious.

WARNING SIGNS

BEHAVIOURAL STRESS SYMPTOMS

- increased smoking
- increased drinking
- overeating
- eating only minimal amounts
- eating nothing at all
- neglecting personal appearance
- driving aggressively
- shutting yourself off from others
- starting lots of things without finishing anything (chores at home, office work)

- nail-biting
- hair-pulling
- skin-picking
- having obsessive thoughts and ideas
- compulsive actions (checking and re-checking locks, lights, taps, etc.)

SUCCESSFUL STRESS MANAGEMENT

CASE HISTORY: COMPULSIVE BEHAVIOUR

Julia (28) had been going out with Mark for two years. They did not live together but saw each other several times a week. After two very unsatisfactory relationships Julia was overjoyed to have found a person she felt she was compatible with.

Everything went well until Mark started cutting down on their weekly dates, explaining that he was overloaded with work because a colleague had suddenly fallen ill. When this situation continued for over four weeks Julia became anxious and noticed that she felt compelled to check and re-check her locks and windows whenever she left the house. Even if she had already checked twice, she always found that she had to return to the house and check again, even if this meant coming back from the bus stop. She felt something dreadful would happen unless she went back and checked again, but she could not say what this disaster might be.

In her hypnotherapy sessions, Julia learned to relax physically and mentally. In addition, she gained an understanding of the root cause of her compulsive symptoms. It turned out that both of Julia's previous relationships had ended because her former partners had been unfaithful to her, both claiming that they had too much to do at work when, in reality, they were meeting other women. So when Mark said a similar thing, alarm bells went off in Julia's mind. Even though she understood on a logical level that Mark was genuine in what he told her, on an emotional level she became very anxious that she would have to go through the trauma of separating once again. Her compulsive action of checking and re-checking was a subconscious protective mechanism that was meant to ward off the impending disaster of Mark leaving her.

In her sessions Julia worked through her experiences in her previous relationships and compared them to her present one with Mark. Julia also finally explained to Mark about her feelings and found him very understanding and helpful. He offered to give her a quick ring from work in the evenings to reassure her and promised to make a special effort to see her more often as soon as work permitted.

Julia was reassured by this and, after five sessions, she noticed a marked reduction in her compulsive behaviour. After eight weeks she was back to her old self again.

(More about the methods Julia used can be found on *page 119* [hypnotherapy]; *page 69* [mental relaxation]; *page 64* [physical relaxation] and *page 92* [addressing problems].)

QUESTIONNAIRE: WHAT IS YOUR STRESS LEVEL?

The following questionnaire has been divided up into five sections, encompassing body and mind, your personality, circumstances, work life, and home life. Each category has its own score and assessment at the end.

Answer the questions without spending too much time thinking about them; there are no right or wrong answers. There is also no point in cheating – no one except yourself will see your score. Remember that the more you know about which areas of your life are causing you stress, the faster you can take positive action and deal with them.

A: YOUR BODY AND MIND

This section is concerned with the state of your body and mind over the past six months. The answers to these questions will give you a good idea of your current state of mental and physical health.

Assign points as follows: Never (0 pts) Sometimes (1 pt) Often (2 pts) Always (3 pts)

Over the past six months:

1 Have you had problems going to sleep or staying asleep, or have you found yourself waking up too early? *y*

2 Have you felt nervous, fidgety or tense? *y*

3 Have you had eating problems such as overeating or being unable to eat? *y*

4 Have you had any dizzy spells? *y*

5 Have you had palpitations (i.e. your heart racing) while you are resting? *y*

6 Have you had an upset stomach? *y*

7 Have you noticed uncharacteristic personality changes in yourself, such as getting tearful easily or getting annoyed easily? *y*

8 Have you felt physically exhausted? *y*

9 Have you felt like throwing it all in and leaving? *y*

10 Have you noticed any aches and pains? *y*

RESULTS

Low Stress Level: Under 10 Points
Keep an eye on your symptoms. Even though they may not be acute at the moment, you need to be aware that they can become more serious if you do not deal with them.

Medium Stress Level: 10 – 19 Points
You need to take action soon in order to prevent stress from escalating. Start implementing some positive changes (*see Part III*) within the next few days.

High Stress Level: 20 – 30 Points

You may want to see your doctor for a general check-up. Your body and mind are under enormous pressure and you could risk a breakdown unless you take these symptoms seriously.

B: YOUR PERSONALITY

This section deals with your attitudes, beliefs and predispositions – important factors when it comes to dealing with stress. Please answer either 'yes' or 'no', scoring 2 points for each 'yes' and 0 points for each 'no'.

1 Are you easily hurt by criticism? *y*

2 Are you often anxious and afraid? *y*

3 Do you find it difficult to express anger in a constructive way? *n*

4 Do you generally put other people's needs before your own? *y*

5 Do you often feel out of control and powerless? *y*

6 Do you feel guilty when you are not working? *y*

7 Are you a perfectionist and excessively conscientious? *y*

8 Are you frequently depressed? *y*

9 Do you feel that others are taking advantage of you? *n*

10 Are you often worried about what others think of you? *y*

RESULTS

Low Stress Level: 2 – 4 Points

Even though you have only said 'yes' to one or two of the questions, please deal with these issues, especially if your problem areas are anxiety and depression.

Medium Stress Level: 6 – 8 Points

The quality of your life will be greatly enhanced once you have dealt with your lack of confidence. Think about going to assertiveness classes, or start using some of the self-help methods in this book (*see page 87*).

High Stress Level: 12 – 20 Points

You may find that the quickest way of overcoming your anxiety and lack of confidence is by going to see a therapist or getting some other form of outside help.

C: YOUR CIRCUMSTANCES

This section deals with life changes that have occurred over the last 18 months. Please answer either 'yes' or 'no', scoring 2 points for each 'yes' and 0 points for each 'no'.

Over the last 18 months:

1 Have you been made redundant? *y*

2 Have you encountered financial difficulties? *n*

3 Has someone near to you had an accident, fallen gravely ill or died? *n*

4 Have you moved house? *y*

5 Have you had a new baby or acquired stepchildren through marriage? *n*

6 Have you contracted a serious disease or had an accident? *n*

7 Have you got married? *y*

8 Have you changed to a new line of work? *y*

9 Have you been promoted? *n*

10 Has your relationship with your partner broken up? ∩

RESULTS

Low Stress Level: Up to 4 Points

Your circumstances will affect you according to your personality. If you had a low stress score in section B of this questionnaire, you are likely to take life changes in your stride. If your score in section B was high, 2 – 4 points in this section may catapult you into the medium (or even high) stress level.

Medium Stress Level: 6 – 10 Points

You have a lot on your plate, even though some of the changes may be positive. Please look after yourself.

High Stress Level: 12 – 20 Points

Make sure you get as much support from family and friends as you can to help you cope.

D: YOUR WORK

The following questions should be answered in respect of the last 12 months. If you do not work, please look at the end of this section for some questions that address your situation more specifically.

Assign points as follows: Never (0 pts) Sometimes (1 pt) Often (2 pts) Always (3 pts)

Over the last 12 months:

1 Have you had to deal with hostility from colleagues, your boss or your customers/clients? ∩

2 Have you been under threat of redundancy? ∩

3 Have you had to cope with sexual harassment? *n*

4 Has there been a tense atmosphere at work? *y*

5 Have you had to work with inadequate equipment? *n*

6 Have you had to work overtime? *y*

7 Have office politics prevented you from doing your work well? *y*

8 Have you had insufficient support from your colleagues or your superiors? *n*

9 Have you felt isolated at work? *n*

10 Have paperwork and/or too many meetings stopped you from doing what you were supposed to do? *y*

RESULTS

Low Stress Level: Up to 10 Points
Your work situation seems reasonably under control, with only the occasional hiccups.

Medium Stress Level: 11 – 19 Points
There appears to be an unhealthy accumulation of stress producing situations at your place of work. Is there anything you can do about these problems, by being more assertive for example? Or do you need to look for another job?

High Stress Level: 20 – 30 Points
Your work environment is a health hazard. You should seriously consider taking matters up with your superiors, or changing jobs.

If you are retired or unemployed:

- Are you happy with your situation?: 0 points (*see* Low Stress Level, above)
- Are you struggling with it?: 15 points (*see* Medium Stress Level, above)
- Do you feel life has lost meaning because of it?: 30 points (*see* High Stress Level, above)

E: YOUR HOME LIFE

This section includes issues such as relationship problems within your family, as well as your living environment.

Assign points as follows: Never (0 pts) Sometimes (1 pt) Often (2 pts) Always (3 pts)

In the last 12 months:

1 Have you felt unsafe or threatened in your home or outside it?

2 Have you had serious problems with your children?

3 Have you had rows or difficulties with your neighbours?

4 Have you had to put up with noise or air pollution in your neighbourhood?

5 Have you had insufficient emotional or practical support from your partner or family?

6 Have you felt lonely and isolated?

7 Have you felt unappreciated by your partner or family?

8 Has your career been in conflict with that of your partner?

9 Has your partner displayed symptoms of stress?

10 Have you experienced sexual problems, including a lack of a sexual partner or a sexually over-demanding partner? *n*

RESULTS

Low Stress Level: Up to 10 Points
Especially if you have answered 'often' or 'always' to one or two questions, the issues concerned will need attention. If, however, you have accumulated your points by saying 'sometimes' to a few questions, your home life appears to be reasonably OK.

Medium Stress Level: 11 – 19 Points
It may be useful to sit down with your family and see how matters can be resolved. Be sure to take some positive action to prevent your stress levels from increasing.

High Stress Level: 20 – 30 Points
Your home life is severely jeopardized by a number of issues. Seek outside help if necessary.

Now that you have gone through all the individual sections of this questionnaire, you will have noticed in which areas of your life you scored highly.

In order to evaluate your overall stress level, you should now add up the scores of all five categories. Remember to add the special scores if you are unemployed or retired.

OVERALL RESULT

Up to 37 points
Your overall stress level is not too bad (if less than 25) and still manageable in the figures approaching 37.

38 – 77 points

Any figure over 70 is already in the danger zone. Your stress levels need urgent attention! Below 70, some constructive management could make a great difference to the quality of your life.

78 – 130 points

If your score is over 100, you are heading for a breakdown unless you take positive steps NOW, but even if between 78 and 100, make sure you take action soon.

PART 3

... AND HOW TO CLIMB OUT OF THE STRESS TRAP

Having looked at the causes and symptoms of stress in the first two parts of this book, we now come to some solutions. It is all well and good to understand the issues that are creating inner pressure for you and how this pressure manifests itself, but ultimately the crucial question is 'How can I get rid of the pressure?'

As you have read in preceding chapters, excessive stress is not just an unpleasant psychological experience, it is also harmful physically, emotionally and mentally.

In the chapters that follow you will find practical methods and techniques of combating stress. Clearly detailed exercises will help you get to grips with your particular problem area. Provided you practise the techniques regularly, you will soon get some relief from your stress symptoms. However, just *reading* about the techniques will not have any effect – some effort is required on your part!

Please take your stress symptoms seriously. We cannot always choose our circumstances, but we can certainly choose to deal with them in a constructive manner. Take action, and take it now. Waiting for 'the right time' is a tricky business – the right time may never come, and while you are waiting around without doing anything your stress symptoms can grow out of proportion and take over your life. Better to deal with your stress while you are still in control than to let your stress control you. It is not really that hard; it just takes some determination and some practice.

HOW TO STOP YOURSELF FROM OVERWORKING

One of the most common causes of stress is overworking. Even though certain jobs entail a great deal of work by their very nature, not everyone who holds such a job feels stressed. This means that it is not the job itself that creates the stress, but rather the individual's attitude towards that job. People often create their own stress by refusing to ask for help when they are overloaded, by failing to delegate or by taking on more than they can cope with. These mistakes are made by people in all walks of life: managers, foremen, teachers, housewives, the self-employed, mothers – all can be guilty of creating unnecessary stress for themselves.

Overworking can also become a compulsion. This can happen after a period of genuine work overload, after which the person finds that he or she is unable to re-adjust to normality. Instead, he or she stays in overdrive, incapable of leaving any work unfinished and reluctant to take any breaks. If you are a compulsive worker, you will *make* work when there is no work. A good indication of a compulsive tendency is feeling incapable of going to bed even though you are exhausted or ill, without first finishing some trivial job like tidying up.

Even though workaholics know that they should take it easier, they find it difficult to slow down. They are forever wanting 'just to do that one other thing'; one thing leads to the next, and before they know it they have worked through their lunch break again.

If you can identify with some of these traits, ask yourself the following questions:

A Whom are you trying to please by working so hard?

B Do you find it difficult to ask for help?

Let us look at each question in turn.

A: WHOM ARE YOU TRYING TO PLEASE?

People coming from a family background where there was great emotional pressure to perform well to gain parental approval can develop in one of two ways. They either drop out altogether or they keep on striving for their parents' approval by working extraordinarily hard, even after their parents have died. What was in childhood experienced as unpleasant pressure has now become a necessity. They can only feel a sense of self-esteem when they stick to the old rules their parents made – 'you are only worth while if you work incessantly.' Therefore, taking breaks or delegating work becomes impossible if they are to keep their self-respect.

SOLUTIONS
- Be aware that adults have a right to make their own rules, provided these rules do not harm anyone else. This means that you are entitled to make your own rules and relegate your parents' rules to the past.
  - You can choose to prioritize.
  - You can choose to delegate.

– You can choose to ask for help.
– You can choose to take your physical and emotional needs seriously.

• If you cannot make these choices without feeling very guilty, get professional help from a counsellor, psychotherapist or hypnotherapist. You will be surprised how much more there is to life than work!

Another group of people who overwork are those who were ignored by their parents. Consequently, they work extra hard to prove to themselves that they are 'somebody' after years of being treated as 'nobody'. They validate themselves through their work.

SOLUTIONS

• Work on your relationships. Make sure you surround yourself with people who like you so you get positive feedback about yourself. Work on your confidence so you can go out and meet new people and find those who are on your wavelength.

• If you feel you lack interpersonal skills, work on developing them by going on a course that teaches methods to overcome your inhibitions.

B: PROBLEMS ASKING FOR HELP

If you have been made to feel incompetent or a nuisance when you needed help in the past, you may now be reluctant to ask when you need something, for fear of being rejected. Coupled with a shy personality, this emotional baggage from the past can become a stumbling block later on. The fear is often that you will inconvenience people.

SOLUTION

- Give others a chance to show that they are helpful. Unless you ask them for help when you need it, you will never find out who your true friends are. Apart from anything else, it is also unfair to others to consider them unhelpful without having any proof of this.

Some people find it generally difficult to admit that they cannot cope, and therefore feel they would be admitting a weakness if they asked someone to help them. They are also worried that others might use this knowledge about their 'weakness' against them at some later point, so they prefer to battle on by themselves, even until they drop with exhaustion.

SOLUTIONS

- Bear in mind that when you ask for help in a professional matter, the focus of attention is the project in hand, not you. Phrase your request accordingly: 'If we want to finish this project on time, I will need some extra help' – not, 'I don't know, I just don't seem to be able to cope. Can you help me?'
- When you ask for help in a personal context, and as long as you ask in a reasonable manner, you are unlikely to be refused very often. If you are, you might want to re-examine your relationship with that particular person.

Another category of people are those who are mistrustful of others. These are usually perfectionists who doubt that anyone else can do a job as well as they can, so they never delegate. In addition, perfectionists in managerial positions will want to check in detail and control what other people are doing, which then results in an even greater workload for them, with the added disadvantage that their subordinates feel put out by this heavy supervision.

- Perfectionism is born out of fear and insecurity. A truly confident person can be thorough but flexible in his or her approach to work. Consider working on building your confidence.

Finally, there are those who believe 'it doesn't count unless I do it all myself.' These are very ambitious people, often workaholics, who feel they gain status if they are perceived to handle everything themselves. Interestingly, this category often contains people who genuinely thrive on a hectic environment. The only problem with this is that it can sometimes lead to them overshooting the limit between enjoying a challenge and damaging their health.

SOLUTION

- Watch out for signs that tell you that you are approaching the dividing line between pleasure and pain. These signs could include smoking or drinking too much to get through the day, or any physical aches and pains. Please respect this threshold. Remember, it is not going to do your status any good if you collapse in a heap!

SO YOU THOUGHT
YOU KNEW HOW
TO BREATHE ...

We breathe day and night, 24 hours a day, whether we are aware of it or not. Although we can consciously control our breathing, it is generally an unconscious activity. Every time we breathe in, the ribs and muscles of the chest wall, as well as the diaphragm (a dome-shaped muscular structure that separates the chest cavity from the abdominal area) help in the expansion and contraction of the lungs and distribute oxygen from the air into the bloodstream. Every time we breathe out, carbon dioxide is expelled from our lungs. The movements of breathing are regulated by several nerve centres in the brain. Cells in the brain stem are believed to control the rhythm and depth of breathing, while the *vagus*, or tenth cranial nerves control the blood vessels and bronchi of the lungs. Because the body stores practically no oxygen, any interference with breathing manifests immediately as a physical symptom such as dizziness, nausea or headaches, chest pains, shortness of breath or even fainting.

Even though the autonomic nervous system (our inner 'autopilot') keeps us breathing automatically without us having to attend to it consciously, our breathing is extremely susceptible to interference. According to what mood we are in, how we are feeling and how these feelings change, our breathing will be fast or slow, regular or irregular, deep or shallow. When you have just lifted something heavy or finished your workout routine, you are puffing and panting, your breathing coming in rapid bursts, the emphasis on the out-breaths. When you dive into water head first you hold your breath for a few seconds – just as you do when you are startled by a sudden loud noise or when someone insults you. And here we come to the relevance of breathing in the context of stress. As you experience any physical or emotional strain it will immediately affect your breathing, often in a detrimental way. Whether you are overworked, feel threatened or frustrated, or are forced to work or live with unpleasant people, your distress will be reflected in your breathing. At times of stress your breathing becomes irregular and shallow, with overlong periods during which you involuntarily hold your breath. This means that not enough oxygen gets to the brain, and this ultimately leads to an inability to concentrate, dizziness and a general feeling of agitation.

Generally, this unhealthy breathing pattern redresses itself once the stressful event has passed, but often just *remembering* that same event later on can disturb your breathing once more. This is why traumatic events in childhood are often held as a faulty breathing pattern for years afterwards, sometimes all the way into adulthood. It is as if the shock of past trauma was so great that neither body nor mind is able to let go and re-adjust to non-stressed thinking and breathing. In these cases, psychotherapy or counselling can help address the past trauma that is causing stress in the present, and as these issues are being dealt with your breathing pattern can return to normal again.

However, in most cases where breathing is adversely affected by stress it can be sorted out by some common-sense strategies which include dealing with the stress-inducing situation and consciously adjusting your breathing so that it can return to normal again. Before we look at a few exercises that will enable you to influence your breathing positively, I would like you to test whether you breathe correctly.

TEST

- Lie down on your back, either on your bed or on the floor. Rest your head on a small pillow or a rolled up towel to give it support. Loosen any belt or tight waistband you may be wearing.

- Place one hand on your chest and the other hand on your belly area.

- Spend a few minutes lying still while you listen to a radio programme to distract yourself from your breathing.

- Once your body has settled down, begin to focus your attention on your hands and begin to observe which of your hands is being pushed up regularly by your in-breaths.

If the hand on your *chest* is moving up and down, this means that your diaphragm stays stiff as you breathe and is therefore only permitting the top part of your lungs to be filled with air. This means that a great deal less oxygen is available to go to your internal organs, including your brain. At the same time not enough carbon dioxide is being expelled from your body, which negatively influences metabolism. Also, the lack of movement in the diaphragm means that both your liver and heart are insufficiently stimulated because the 'massaging' effect of diaphragmatic movement is absent. This results in insufficient circulation in your liver and heart.

If the hand on your *belly* is moving up and down, this means that the top half of your lungs are not sufficiently 'aired' because most of the oxygen is going down into the bottom part of your lungs. Generally, breathing mainly through your belly

area is better than breathing through your chest only, simply because the diaphragm is more mobile. The disadvantage, however, is that you never breathe out properly and that the chest area is never exercised to its full potential.

If both your hands, one after the other, rise and fall as you breathe, then you are breathing correctly. Air is flowing into the lower part of the lungs first (hand on belly rises) and then spreading into the upper part (hand on chest rises). On breathing out, the air moves from the chest area down into the belly region as it is expelled (hand on chest sinking down marginally earlier than hand on belly).

When you breathe correctly, two processes happen simultaneously as you inhale – your ribcage expands and your diaphragm presses down. This creates increased space in the trunk of your body, permitting the lungs to expand. This process is reversed during exhalation – the ribcage contracts again and the diaphragm moves up so that the lungs deflate and air is expelled.

Choose one of the following exercises depending on whether you need to improve your lower or your upper lung activity.

INCREASING LOWER LUNG ACTIVITY
(BELLY AREA)

- Lie down comfortably, loosen tight clothing and put one hand on your belly above your navel.

- Tighten up your stomach and belly muscles so that they tuck in.

- Relax your belly muscles again and feel the difference between tension and relaxation in this area.

- Repeat this exercise five times to heighten your awareness of your belly area.

– Rest for a moment and allow your breathing to go whichever way it wants to go. It does not matter whether you breathe quickly or slowly, regularly or irregularly.

Now continue as follows:

– Place one hand on your belly. Inhale in such a way that the hand on your belly is pushed upwards.

– Breathe out through your mouth, making a long 'HAAAA' sound as you do so. Notice how your belly area deflates and how this makes your hand go down again.

– Repeat this exercise ten times.

Whenever you have a spare moment, be it waiting in a queue at the supermarket or sitting at traffic lights in your car, use this time to breathe consciously through your belly area.

– Every once in a while, breathe in so that your belly extends out while at the same time creating some counter-pressure by pressing your hand on your belly. This helps strengthen the belly muscles which, perhaps as a result of not having been used for a long time, may have become weak.

– This exercise should be repeated five times if possible and can be done anywhere, any time, sitting or standing up.

(There is another exercise to co-ordinate belly and chest breathing, which is on *page 61* after the exercises to train chest breathing.)

- Lie down comfortably, loosen tight clothing and spread both arms, fully extended, on the floor so that your body forms a cross, your arms making the horizontal line to the vertical line of the rest of your body. Notice how opening your arms out like this creates more space in your chest cavity.

- Now fold your arms tightly over your chest, as if hugging yourself. Notice how this constricts the space your chest has available.

- Repeat this exercise five times.

Take a break for a few minutes, then continue as follows:

- Repeat the exercise, but this time breathe in as you open your arms out and breathe out as you fold them over your chest.

- Repeat this exercise ten times.

Use any lull in activity during the day to take in a few deep breaths through your chest.

Only when you can do the first two exercises easily should you go on to the third exercise, which is the same for both groups. This exercise can be done lying down, sitting up or standing.

CO-ORDINATING UPPER AND
LOWER LUNG ACTIVITY

- Breathe in through your belly area, then let the air fill the chest cavity as well. Do this as smoothly as possible – imagine a wave spreading from the bottom of your lungs to the top.

- Practise this until you can do it effortlessly. In the meantime don't worry about your out-breaths.

– Now co-ordinate your in-breath and your out-breath. Breathe in correctly and allow the air to escape from the top of your lungs first before the belly area 'deflates'.

– Practise this until you can do it smoothly.

– Practise correct breathing three times a day for at least two weeks so that this new, better habit can become more firmly established.

The reason why it makes sense to work on your breathing is two-fold – correct breathing can prevent you from getting stressed in the first place, and it can also help you regain control more quickly once you are stressed.

Body and mind work as a unit. When the body becomes stressed through illness, injury or excessive demand, this will have a direct knock-on effect on the mind. Depending on your personal disposition, a physical overload can express itself as tearfulness, irritability, indecisiveness or depression. Accordingly, your ability to work efficiently will be influenced, and this in turn will be reflected in the results you are getting.

Just as the body influences the mind, so the mind has an effect on the body. If you are of an anxious disposition and have a tendency to worry and spend a lot of time going through disaster scenarios in your mind, you not only exacerbate your anxiety but also force your body into constant overdrive. As you fret over things that have gone wrong in the past and things that may go wrong in the future, you force your body to adapt to the warning signals your mind is sending out. Your body cannot distinguish whether an unpleasant situation is real or imagined; it switches into overdrive regardless. Blood-pressure goes up, heart rate increases, digestion slows down and adrenalin is released; all the muscles tense up to get ready for 'fight or flight'. If your body is subjected to prolonged or repeated muscle tension caused by anxiety, the consequence can be headaches, back and neck problems, and breathing difficulties.

Correct breathing enables your body to relax and regain its natural equilibrium, at the same time calming your mind and making you feel in control again so that your anxiety (and its related symptoms) can abate.

GIVING YOUR BODY TIME OFF

A s stress is linked to such a formidable number of physical reactions, it makes sense to help your body regain its balance during and after any stressful period. Although bodily stress reactions are aroused within a split second, they need a much longer time to fade away again. This is where conscious support and assistance can speed up the recovery process.

Any relief you provide for your body will also positively influence your mind and emotions, even though your mind may have created the stress in the first place. In the previous chapter you have read about training your breathing so that you maintain a balanced intake of oxygen, especially when you are under pressure. Now I would like to explain how you can relax more deeply. You will find the exercises in this section particularly valuable if you have sleeping problems.

When lots of things are going on around you and you are whizzing about, trying to juggle dozens of chores at the same time, you may feel that you have no time to stop. You may feel that if you were to stop you would lose valuable time which could be better put to decreasing the mountains of work that surround you. When you operate like this, without resting, you are no longer in control of your work – your work is in control of you. A short burst of herculean energy is OK, but it can never be a good long-term strategy. As you fire on all cylinders over a prolonged period of time, you eventually end up running on empty, and once a physical or emotional breakdown has occurred it takes a long time for body and mind to recover. This is why it makes sense to allow yourself some rest intermittently while you are going through a stressful period, not just to protect your body from undue exhaustion but also to keep a perspective on the matters you have to attend to.

ALLOWING YOURSELF TO REST

Once you have finished one chunk of work, take a break of five to ten minutes. Here are some suggestions:

- Have a bite to eat. Do this *sitting down*, and have the food *on a plate*, even if you are only having three biscuits and an apple. Eating while standing over the sink or by the fridge does not count!

- If at all possible, remove yourself from your working environment for a moment. Go outside, do a breathing exercise, or walk around the block. A change of scenery, combined with gentle physical exercise, allows the body's stress responses to simmer down and thereby preserves your energy.

- Withdraw to somewhere quiet for a moment. If there are many people working around you, find somewhere away from the noise, even if it is only the toilet. Close your eyes for a few moments and allow your body to rest.

- If you are working from home, put on a favourite piece of music. It does not have to be slow or quiet, so long as it relaxes you. Sit or lie down with your eyes closed and listen for a little while. Notice how your body begins to unwind.

If your day really offers you no opportunity to unwind, follow any of these suggestions once your day's work is done. As this will mean that you have worked throughout the day without a proper break, you will have to make the evening break considerably longer to achieve the same result.

In addition to the short breaks suggested above, here are some more comprehensive ways of helping your body to relax:

GIVING YOUR BACK A TREAT

– Lie down on the floor or on a firm bed. Loosen any tight clothing.

– Support your head with a cushion or a rolled up towel.

– Pull your knees up so that your feet are flat on the floor (or bed), hip-width apart, your knees pointing towards the ceiling.

– Let your hands rest on your hips, arms flat on the floor or bed.

– Feel the lower part of your back making contact with the floor or bed.

– Close your eyes and remain in this position as you (slowly) count to 20.

– Now bring your knees up to your chest and hug your legs in towards you. Keep your eyes closed and hold this position to the count of 20. Feel how your lower back pushes even further into the floor or bed beneath you.

– Go back to the original position and repeat the entire process twice more.

This exercise relaxes your back because lying down relieves the pressure put on the intervertebral discs by gravity. This pressure shortens the back muscles so that fluid is squeezed out from between the discs. By lying down, you take pressure off your back and allow these muscles to relax. As your lower back sinks down onto the floor or bed, the spine lengthens and allows fluid to re-enter the centre of the discs, restoring the cushioning effect of the fluid on the discs.

LOOSENING MUSCLES

- Lie down on the floor or on a firm bed; loosen tight clothing.

- Support your head with a small cushion. Allow your legs and arms to lie loosely stretched out, arms next to your body. If you suffer from lower back problems, put a thickly rolled up blanket under the back of your knees.

- Close your eyes and tense your feet and lower legs. Hold the tension to the slow count of five. Now release the tension again, repeating in your mind the words, 'Heavy and heavier, sinking deeper' and, if you can, imagine the muscles in your feet and calves relaxing down into the floor or mattress.

- Take a deep breath in through your nose, hold it for a moment and then exhale slowly through your mouth, making a 'HAAAA' sound as you do so.

- Give yourself a moment to feel the relaxation in your feet and lower legs.

- Now continue with your thighs and buttocks. Tense them up tightly to the slow count of five, then release the tension again, thinking, 'Heavy and heavier, sinking deeper' repeatedly as you let go. Visualize the tension drifting away.

- Take in a deep breath again, hold it and release it as before.

68   Feel the relaxation in your feet, legs and buttocks.

- Continue in the same manner for your belly area, your chest, hands, arms and shoulders together, and finally your face (grit your teeth and frown).

- Remain calmly resting on the floor or bed for a while afterwards. You may even drift off to sleep for a moment or two, so if you have other things to do later set your alarm clock before you begin this exercise.

This exercise has a highly relaxing effect because it systematically releases all the tension in your body. You may not have noticed yourself tensing up during the day because you have been too focused on the job that needed doing, maybe worrying whether you could finish it on time. By the time evening comes your body feels stiff and painful. Typical stress-aches are in the head, neck or shoulders, and if your stress persists during the night you may find that your jaw aches next morning because you have been grinding your teeth in your sleep. The systematic release of tension as described in this exercise helps your body to relax fully, and this will also help you sleep better.

TAKING A MENTAL
HOLIDAY

To relax the body is one thing; to relax the mind is quite another and poses its own challenges. Whereas the body reacts quite readily to mechanical exercises like tensing and relaxing, the mind is much less easy to control. Thoughts are like a bunch of slippery eels – as you close your fingers around them they slither away and proceed to wriggle around all over the place ...

Hopefully you will have used the muscle-loosening exercise (*page 67*) and will have noticed how it encourages you to use your mind in two ways. First, you are asked to think certain thoughts ('heavy and heavier, sinking deeper'), then you are asked to imagine what your muscles look like as they are relaxing. Both the suggestive thoughts and the visualization keep your mind occupied as you relax your body. If you were to leave your mind unoccupied it would very likely start wandering off and worrying about what other jobs need doing after you have finished the exercise, or worse, about what has gone wrong during the day. These unsettling thoughts not only disturb your concentration so that you are distracted from your exercise, they also counteract any efforts to relax – worry creates physical tension. It is therefore better to keep your thoughts busy in a productive fashion.

Controlling your mind takes know-how and quite a bit of practice, and some people are better at it than others. In times of stress, reining in your mind's negative meanderings is crucial, and the best way of doing so is through mental images, also known as visualization. You do not have to be creative or have any particular psychic powers to visualize successfully; all you need is an everyday ability to daydream. When you are looking forward to your next holiday, you can already see yourself in your mind's eye sitting on the beach or on the terrace of your hotel, sipping a drink. Equally, past events can create pictures in your mind. Visualization is just as straightforward.

You can test your ability to visualize with the following exercise.

MAKING PICTURES IN YOUR MIND

With your eyes closed, imagine

– a house

– a garden

– a street.

Take your time. Look at each image carefully. What sort of house are you thinking of? A country or a town house? A bungalow or one with two or more storeys? Modern or old-fashioned? Is your garden formal or informal? Well-kept or neglected? What sort of plants are in it? Is it a garden you know, or one you have never seen before? What sort of houses are in your street? Are there any shops?

Once you have spent a little time exploring each image, you should be able to describe it to someone else.

When you go through this exercise you will notice that visualizing is not quite the same thing as seeing with your eyes open. Whereas you get a sharp, focused picture that remains steady when your eyes are open, mental images tend to be much more fluid, more like *ideas* of what something looks like rather than an unchanging reproduction of reality.

In order to achieve mental relaxation during stressful periods, use either of the following two exercises during any breaks you are able to take. The exercises also lend themselves to being done directly after you have completed loosening your muscles as described on *page 67*.

ACCESSING PAST RELAXATION

Even though you are stressed at the moment, there will have been times when you have been very relaxed. This could have been on your last holiday or when you last visited good friends. You may even have memories of childhood when you happily played outdoors, feeling relaxed and safe.

– Settle down in a chair or lie down. Close your eyes and allow your mind to wander back to the time when you had peace of mind.

– Remember in as much detail as possible. If your relaxing memory is of a past holiday, recall the location, the scenery, the people and the particular occasion when you felt so calm and comfortable.

– Remain in the memory as long as you can. Dwell on it, enjoy it and draw it out.

– One way of prolonging the exercise is by seeking out other memories that are of a similar nature, other times when you felt safe and relaxed and happy with life, and link them with the first memory that came to your mind.

The more details you can collect, the more your mind becomes focused on the task and the more you become immersed in the process of remembering. This will automatically result in a deepening of your physical relaxation as well as a lifting of your mood.

CREATING A RELAXING IMAGE

You may be momentarily unable to access any relevant memories, or perhaps the last relaxing episode in your life occurred so long ago that you cannot remember it in enough detail to make it sufficiently powerful to relax you now. If this is the case, you can simply invent a relaxing scenario.

– Before you get started, choose from one of the following words the one that you associate most with the notion of relaxation: calmness, peace, tranquillity, serenity, quiet, harmony, or stillness.

– Sit or lie down comfortably and close your eyes.

– Repeat your chosen word in your mind. Do so *with feeling*. Do this slowly, and say the word over and over again until an image begins to emerge that fits the meaning of your word. This may be a real-life scenario such as of walking through beautiful countryside, or it may be a fantasy image such as of drifting along with the clouds in the sky, high above the hustle and bustle of the world.

– Embroider your scenario as much as you like in order to prolong the process of staying with your relaxing image.

– Involve all your senses in your image – sight, sound, touch and smell. The more detailed the image, the better its relaxing effect on your body and mind.

You can change scenarios if you wish, or you can stick to the same one every time you want to relax mentally. Some people have a favourite scene that they know will relax them; others need to alternate between several lest they get bored. Whatever works for you is the right thing to do.

In some ways, this type of mental relaxation is like meditation if we understand meditating as a process of concentrating on one particular thing to the exclusion of all others. It is really a process of selective attention, very much like what happens in hypnosis. The aim of transcendental meditation is to empty the mind of all thought. This requires virtually decades of practice, whereas the exercises here are easy to master – all you are required to do is to focus on a remembered or constructed relaxing image. Of course you will still have to put some practice in to get good results next time you feel stressed out, so start practising now!

SLEEPING BETTER

How well you sleep will greatly depend on the state of mind you are in before you go to bed. Anyone who worries a lot knows how difficult it can be to drop off to sleep while your mind is still busy with unsettling thoughts.

A good night's sleep is a valuable antidote to stress and the most effective way to rest body and mind. Also, the process of dreaming allows your subconscious mind to deal with the day's events and to work through them, which is vital for maintaining mental health. So when stress disrupts your sleep, this sets up a vicious circle – because you sleep less well, you lack concentration the next day; this in turn reduces your ability to cope with any problems you may encounter during the day, resulting in more worry, more stress and a second night of disturbed sleep … Sleep is often elusive when you need it most.

The biological explanation to stress-induced insomnia is that the excess of adrenalin generated by worrying is still active in the body when it is time to go to sleep. During sleep, the body produces growth hormones which help renew body tissue, but these hormones can only work in the absence of adrenalin. This is why it is important to stick to a reasonably regular bedtime routine, allowing adrenalin levels to subside so that the regenerating growth hormones can do their work while you are asleep.

In this context it is not how many hours of sleep you get that is important, but rather that you get good quality sleep. There is really no ideal number of hours – some people function effectively on as little as four, others need up to ten hours to wake up refreshed. Provided you go to sleep easily, stay asleep during the night and wake up feeling good, you are getting enough sleep.

Most people will have experienced insomnia at one time or another. The sleep you get the night before an exam or before a visit to the dentist's can be disrupted, or the excitement about a holiday beginning the next day can affect your sleeping pattern. In most cases this pattern returns to normal once the big event is over. Problems occur, however, when the disrupted sleeping pattern becomes self-perpetuating. If you feel tired but still cannot get to sleep for a long time after going to bed, you are likely to feel anxious about getting enough rest the next night, and it is this very anxiety that stops you from going to sleep.

Sleeping tablets may appear to be the solution, and they can be helpful in the short term, but they are certainly *not* advisable for long-term use. Sleeping tablets can leave you feeling drowsy right through the next day. And unless you are taking herbal sleeping pills, there is also a chance that you may become addicted to the tablets, either physically or psychologically. Then when you finally do decide to stop taking them (always gradually, and always under a doctor's supervision), you may find your insomnia returns worse than ever.

You are better off using some very effective alternatives to tablets which will help you re-establish a good sleeping pattern without any negative side-effects. The exercises that follow will enable you to stop worrying and prepare your body and mind for sleep. These techniques work best if they are preceded by a breathing and relaxation exercise as described on pages 59 and 67.

WORRY-BUSTING

Worrying is like a mini-anxiety that is perpetually nagging at the back of your mind. Bedtime is a particularly fertile period for worry because everything around you is still, you are just lying there, and all your emotions can come to the surface without being deflected by the usual daytime activities. In the evening and at night you are much more exposed to your feelings because you are in that twilight state between waking and sleeping where your conscious mind is no longer fully switched on but you are still awake enough to register thoughts and feelings. In this semi-trance state your mind can get stuck in a 'worry-loop' which keeps you from dropping off to sleep.

MAKING A MENTAL LIST

You will be familiar with the old remedy of counting sheep to induce sleep. This works well for some, but the disadvantage is that it leaves your mind with too much room for manoeuvre, even though the monotony of watching sheep hop over a fence does have a soporific effect. However, when you are worried about something, day-problems tend to intrude on your sheep-counting and disrupt it a little too easily.

Try one of the following alternatives:

- Make a mental list of all the furniture in your house and/or office. If you are still awake after this, continue by making an inventory of the furniture in your parents' house and the homes of your friends and other family members.

- Make a mental list of all the lights and light fittings in your home, in your office, in your parents' home and your friends' homes.

These exercises require some focused attention together with some neutral visualization of locations, and this creates a very effective distraction from everyday worries.

DELEGATE PROBLEMS TO YOUR SUBCONSCIOUS

When Thomas Edison, the inventor, struggled to create the light bulb he relegated questions to his subconscious mind each night before going to sleep. After a few nights the answers came to him. Albert Einstein is said to have used a similar technique to help him solve mathematical problems.

If anything has gone wrong during the day or if you feel anxious about something in the future, delegate the problem to your subconscious.

- Use the following formula, 'I now hand over my worries/this problem to my subconscious mind so it can work on a solution while I am asleep. I am now free to go to sleep.'

- Use this formula every night. You will notice a certain sense of relief that comes with abdicating the solution of problems to a deeper level of your mind during the night – it really does give you a sense of lightness and freedom as you 'unburden' yourself in this way.

- To support this technique further, it can be useful to jot down before you go to bed all the things that need setting right. That way you have a concept and a plan for the next day, which can help you to feel more in control and therefore more relaxed.

CREATE A RELAXING BLANK

When you worry about something at night, you tend to go over the same scenarios again and again, or lose yourself in details about how things could go wrong. This results in a perpetual flow of unsettling thoughts that feed on each other.

To bring this vicious circle to a halt, try the following technique:

- List your worries in a matter of fact way in your mind. Formulate each worry concisely, then say to yourself 'next!' and go on to the next worrying thought.

Here is an example: You are worried about a work meeting the next day.

'My boss may be at his worst tomorrow.' Next! 'He may not like the work I'm presenting.' Next! 'I'm worried that my colleagues might disagree with my findings.' Next! 'Maybe nobody is interested in what I have to say.' Next! 'What if someone asks me a question and I don't know the answer?' Next! etc.

You will be surprised how quickly you come to a point where you cannot think of another worry. This is when you experience a very pleasant blankness in your mind, and this is often when you automatically slip into sleep. If you find yourself going back to worrying after the blank, just repeat the exercise.

PREPARING FOR SLEEP

As already mentioned, you will find it very helpful to do one of the breathing exercises or muscle-relaxation (*see pages 59 and 67*) to prepare your body for sleep.

Here are a few further tips that will make it easier to unwind:

- Avoid vigorous exercise directly before bedtime. Leave at least two hours between aerobic exercise and going to bed.

- Gently stretching your limbs and holding the stretches for one to two minutes helps the relaxation process.

- Sleep in a cool bedroom, but make sure you are comfortably warm in bed.

- Leave at least an hour before you go to bed after your evening meal, but do not go to bed hungry as the hunger pangs will keep you awake.

- Listening to the radio or to taped novels as you lie in bed with your eyes closed is a very effective way of falling asleep – much better than lying in bed with the TV on.

- Have a warm (not hot) bath last thing at night.

- Have a warm herbal tea half an hour before bedtime. Chamomile, valerian or vervain are particularly relaxing.

- Avoid alcohol, caffeine and nicotine, if not altogether than at least for five hours or so before you go to bed.

- Avoid working in bed or discussing domestic or work problems in bed. Treat your bed as your sanctuary, where work issues have no access.

- Establish a reasonably steady bedtime routine, including a certain time when you go to bed and when you get up.

Apart from these general points, you can also use visualization to help you go off to sleep:

- Imagine that you are working in a large hotel with hundreds of bedrooms. Your only job there is to make the beds. In the beginning you still feel fresh and fit, and you make the beds efficiently and quickly. As you continue, though, you grow more and more tired. You begin to slow down. And as you become more exhausted, you begin to wish you could lie down on one of the beds and just drop off to sleep …

Finally, make sure you go to sleep on a positive note:

- Instead of lying in bed reminding yourself of things you could have done or said differently, think of three good things that have happened during the day, no matter how minor. This way you are more likely to go into a deep, satisfying sleep and awake the next day feeling positive.

IF ALL ELSE FAILS

For the hardened insomniac, there is one radical remedy which is tough but works very well within about three to four days if you can persist with it:

- If you go to bed but just cannot get to sleep, get up, get dressed and do some work. (This does not include watching television or listening to the radio). Clean out the kitchen cupboards or deal with some paperwork, write cheques for bills or do anything else that is useful. Only if you cannot keep your eyes open any more, change back into your night clothes and go back to bed. Repeat this procedure as often as necessary. Under no circumstances should you nap during the day while you are trying out this routine at night.

As you can imagine, this routine will be quite uncomfortable because you will be getting very little sleep indeed. At the same time, however, your body and mind will become re-accustomed to a natural day/night rhythm where bed is the place where you sleep rather than toss and turn.

DEALING WITH DIFFICULT PEOPLE

S ometimes we need to interact on a daily basis with colleagues, neighbours or relatives who upset us by the way they speak to us or by their mannerisms. Perhaps you are particularly susceptible to their negative behaviour because your life is not working out as you want it to and their behaviour acts as a trigger, allowing your original upset to spill out. However, there are also genuine cases of people who, through their behaviour, create general discontent and unease. Elsewhere in this book (*page 18*) I have already mentioned some of these difficult people and how they can upset others; now we will address how you can best deal with them.

BULLIES

Bullies will hassle anyone whom they consider weak. If bullies are confronted, however, they usually collapse like a house of cards. This is because they are insecure people who have been bullied themselves as children, either by their parents, siblings, or peers. This may be difficult to believe when you see a bully in action, giving everyone else a hard time. Most people are so intimidated by this display of power that they just put up with it, thinking that it is the quickest way to get rid of the bully. But

82   bullies enjoy seeing you meek and mild; after all, it is the whole point of the exercise. Because bullies themselves have been made to feel powerless in the past, they threaten others; if others show that they are intimidated, this restores the bully's sense of power. Whoever proves to be a good victim to a bully by showing fear will be bullied again and again. This can be a horrendous ordeal for children because the bullying often happens secretly and the victim feels so ashamed of being humiliated that he or she usually does not tell anyone about it.

But bullying is not confined to the playground. It can take quite a sophisticated shape in adults who get their own way by making snide remarks when you prove unable to get to grips with an unreasonable amount of work they have given you, or they may do their bullying in a 'jolly' manner ('Here, let me cook dinner; you won't know how to do it properly.')

SOLUTIONS

Once someone has established a habit of bullying you, he or she won't stop until you show some signs that you are no longer prepared to put up with it.

1 Don't smile any longer at the bully. Many victims try to appease the bully by smiling, but that just marks you out as a victim.

2 Maintain eye contact. This denotes that you are taking back power. It can be quite difficult because most victims of bullying start hating the bully after a while and avert their eyes so that the bully cannot see the resentment there.

3 Whatever you say, don't shout at the bully. Shouting at a bully puts you in a weaker position because you have lost your cool, and this is where the bully wants you anyway.

4 Ask the bully for a private word once you have calmed down. Whether the bully is your boss or your older sister, the issue needs to be addressed before the situation gets out of hand. If you feel very afraid of the bully, you may want to ask a friend or colleague or another family member to come with you to back you up. State clearly that you feel pushed around and that you want this to stop.

BACKSTABBERS

These are people with an inferiority complex who say 'yes' when they really want to say 'no'. They are incapable of voicing their true opinion when they disagree with someone else, especially if the other person is of a higher 'rank' than they are. Sweet as pie while in the presence of the other person, they turn around completely once that person has left the room and begin to make critical or slanderous comments. Backstabbers create stress wherever they go because, even if their criticism of the other person is justified, everyone else grows tired and fed up with the backstabbers' ongoing tirades, which are never supported by any constructive action. It also makes other people wonder (and fear) what the backstabber might be saying about them behind *their* back ...

SOLUTIONS

1 State clearly to the backstabber that you are not interested in gossip. Unless you express this plainly to the backstabber, he or she will assume that you approve. Don't worry that the backstabber will now turn against you – he or she has probably already done so anyway.

2 Point out to the backstabber that any complaints need to be taken up with the person concerned if anything is to change for the better.

3 Leave the room. If a backstabber does not respond to your requests to stop criticizing someone else, you have a right to withdraw from the scene.

4 If you yourself are at the receiving end of backstabbing, do not let it ride. Check carefully what has been said about you. Tell the person who told you about the backstabber's alleged criticism that you will now go and speak to him or her. If people know you will pursue any gossip, this is often enough to get them to stop.

5 Arrange a meeting with the backstabber and ask for an explanation. Make clear that you prefer to be told directly if something is wrong, rather than to hear it from someone else.

SHIRKERS

Shirkers are masters of excuse. Whenever work needs to be done or a helping hand is needed they suddenly remember a dentist's appointment, develop a headache, or claim that their old sports injury is playing up again. Shirkers feel (or pretend to feel) that they are hopelessly overworked, when in reality everyone else is doing double the amount of work in the same time. Shirkers find it very easy to say 'no' to anything that would mean they had to pull their finger out. They behave like spoiled brats, and indeed they have usually been over-indulged as children. They are precious and totally oblivious to other people's needs. If you have to work with a shirker, or if someone in your family is not pulling his or her weight, you are likely to become frustrated after a while because you are the one who does most of the work while the shirkers complain about their impossible workload. If the shirker is your boss you will do all the work while he or she takes all the credit, sometimes without even bothering to mention your name in acknowledgement when the project is completed.

SOLUTIONS

1 Get your facts straight. Take out some time to think carefully whether you are justified in resenting the shirker. Is he or she really not doing enough compared to your own input, or is there a genuine reason why the shirker cannot contribute more?

2 Have a private word. If you are satisfied that the shirker is not pulling his or her weight, speak with him or her and find out if there is some reason you don't know about why the shirker seems unwilling to help. It may be something other than laziness.

3 Describe your position in a constructive way. Explain briefly how the shirker's unhelpful ways affect you. It would be useful if you could say this calmly; you will get better results.

4 Negotiate a better deal. Explain clearly what you need from the shirker to resolve the situation. Negotiate until you can agree on a new plan for working together. You may have to compromise a bit, but remember that any improvement is good news. You can always renegotiate later.

MOANERS

Some people are in the habit of talking endlessly about their own woes. Initially most of us will listen sympathetically to these people. If they have had a hard life, we are usually prepared to listen for quite a while and even to listen repeatedly to the same tales, trying to make constructive suggestions about how they could change things for the better. Sooner or later, however, the time comes when we become exasperated with moaners.

The tell-tale sign that you are dealing with habitual moaners is that these people never take the least interest in your helpful suggestions; it is as if you have not spoken. They just seem to need someone to dump their emotional rubbish on, without ever considering doing something about their problem. Some moaners will be quite ready to appear on your doorstep or at the end of your phone line at any time of night or day, and if you dare complain about this they can even make you feel guilty by saying something like, 'Well, you're just like everyone else, you don't care!' And of course you do not want to be uncaring like all the others, so you continue to listen yet again.

SOLUTIONS

1 Restrict listening time. If you generally like the person, state clearly *before* the moaner launches into another speech that you only have a certain amount of time to listen. If you do not even like the person, you are under no obligation to listen. Do not allow others to treat you as an emotional rubbish dump.

2 Realize that your listening does not help. Many people feel that they can give others relief by letting them go over a problem again and again. This is not always the case, though. Endlessly going over a problem can, on the contrary, have an amplifying effect; the moaner ends up hysterical because the problem is blown out of proportion. You are not helping by listening yet again – you are stopping the moaner from doing something constructive about the problem!

3 Be firm. When moaners accuse you of being uncaring when you ask them to stop moaning, agree with them but insist that you won't listen any more until you see them take positive action. You could say something like, 'I'm sorry if this sounds uncaring to you, but I still don't want you to tell me that story again. Things are not going to improve unless you do something about them.'

USING ANGER CONSTRUCTIVELY

I f you were to ask a hundred people which of their emotions they liked least, the feeling of anger would come quite high on most people's 'dislike-lists'.

Getting angry involves other people; it is triggered by what others say, do, or do not say or do. A display of anger can be observed easily in drivers. Safely tucked into the capsule of their car, some drivers feel a lot less inhibited about showing their annoyance when someone cuts them up on the motorway or commits any other traffic offence. You can see these angry drivers shouting and gesticulating, making rude signals and often driving very aggressively as a consequence. It can be frightening to watch them because you realize that they are beside themselves and out of control so that they do not seem to care what they are doing. Seeing people give way to their anger in this destructive way can indeed make anger look like a most undesirable emotion – yet anger can serve us well, provided we use it constructively.

Why is it that we tend to push anger aside and try our best to ignore it so often? There are a variety of reasons for suppressing anger. For one thing it is considered rude and bad form to show anger openly, so good manners dictate that you pretend nothing has happened, no matter how outrageously you are being treated.

The habit of suppressing anger can also have its roots in childhood. Take the example of growing up in a family where one or both parents has a bad temper. Being exposed to someone who is angry a lot is frightening, and being frightened repeatedly makes you angry, but you have to suppress the anger because you cannot afford to show it – if you did, it would trigger your parents' bad temper and they are stronger than you and could make your life a misery as a consequence.

Anger can also get suppressed when you are criticized or threatened frequently as a child, because this mistreatment erodes self-confidence. In such a set-up, either at home or in school with bullying classmates or teachers, you may very well feel angry at the constant put-downs but at the same time not confident enough to express your anger, so that you are left helpless and frustrated.

Anger can be a valuable feeling which can help resolve situations, provided we use it constructively. Feeling annoyed is the first warning signal that tells us that a situation needs our attention. Let us assume your boss at work has a tendency to give you extra work whenever you are ready to go home. You may feel OK the first time this happens, provided the job is genuinely urgent, but after a few more times you will in all likelihood start feeling put out or annoyed.

At this point many people make the mistake of not saying anything to their boss, but instead go around and complain to all their friends and colleagues about it. The only person who never gets to hear the complaint is the only person who can do something about it – the boss! This is a classic example of unconstructive use of anger.

When something begins to annoy you, it is time to deal with it. At the initial stages of annoyance you are still in control because the feeling of anger is only minor. This means your emotions are not running away with you and you can still think clearly and speak politely. The constructive way of dealing with your annoyance in the example given above would be to speak to your boss and explain that you do not mind doing occasional overtime when it is something urgent, but that it seems to have become a regular event. Can he or she suggest a solution? Maybe a temp could be brought in to help out when there is a work overload?

There is no need for the anger to build up into a big explosion. If anger is not allowed out in a constructive way, it builds up and either you blow your top at a time when it is really inappropriate, or you 'implode', becoming ill or depressed. A build up of anger is a mighty force and it needs to be taken seriously when it is still manageable, otherwise it runs away with you, and not in a direction that you will like very much.

Another type of anger comes from frustration. There are times when you have been struggling with a problem over a long period and are getting heartily fed up with it. Or you may have to deal daily with a situation that exasperates you but which you can genuinely do nothing about. In these cases it can be quite difficult to relax and be positive because your mind keeps wandering off to the problem when you are trying to relax, and with all this emotional interference going on it can be impossible to unwind.

If you are struggling with a frustrating situation or person, you may find it helpful to use the following technique. This 'anger room' technique will allow you to let go of pent-up anger and resentment first so that the path is free for a sensible discussion afterwards. Even if there is nothing that is annoying you at the moment, try out the following exercise – it might come in handy later.

EXERCISE

- Settle back in a comfortable position.

- Close your eyes and think of a frustrating situation or person.

- Now imagine a big room with lots of shelves and several tables in it. Everywhere you look there are stacked-up plates, glasses, bone china and little porcelain figurines.

- Go around the room and begin systematically to smash everything to pieces. Grab a pile of plates and throw them on the floor, hurl glasses against the walls, overturn the tables, and so on. If you want to you can imagine using a big wooden club to do this. Stop only when you have demolished absolutely everything in the room.

- Check how you feel when you have finished.

You should get a feeling of relief after having done this exercise, especially if you have a situation in your life at present that has been frustrating you for a while.

There are a few ground rules which you should observe if you want to use your anger constructively.

1 If you are very angry, do not say anything at all until you have calmed down. You are much more likely to be taken seriously if you remain calm. Do not give the other person an advantage over you by behaving in such a way that he or she can wave off your comments as unreasonable or hysterical ('Is it your time of the month, then?'). This is only going to make you feel more angry, and a shouting match will not resolve the situation.

2 Be honest with yourself. Is it really what this person has said

or done that has created your feeling of annoyance, or does the anger belong somewhere else? Maybe something at work is frustrating you and you are taking it out on your family? Make sure you do not direct your anger at the wrong person.

3 Speak to the other person in private. You may feel like lashing out in public to cause the other person the maximum amount of humiliation, but this is only going to show you in a bad light. It will also make the other person dig in his or her heels so that it becomes even more difficult to resolve the original problem.

4 Before you speak to the other person in private, define for yourself what you want from this conversation. What outcome would be satisfactory for you? What are your expectations concerning the other person's behaviour should a similar situation arise in future? Be clear about your aims or you will have to grapple for words when you are having your private talk.

5 Agree with the other person on a procedure should a similar situation arise again. This means you will both be prepared much better for future occasions.

6 Be prepared to make reasonable concessions. If the other person feels that he or she has come out of the negotiations as the loser, he or she is less likely to stick to your agreement. It is best if you both come away feeling that you have made a fair deal.

7 Only if points 1 – 6 fail, shout!

HOW TO TALK ABOUT THINGS YOU WOULD RATHER AVOID

I t is the things we feel reluctant to talk about that are guaranteed to create emotional stress. The reason we shy away from these issues is that they make us feel uncomfortable or annoyed, and the thought of raising them with someone else frightens and embarrasses us. Unresolved conflict is like a door with two locks on it. Behind the door lies relief, but the door is kept firmly shut by the two locks. One lock is your feelings about the original cause of conflict, for example someone making decisions without asking you even though the decisions affect you. The other lock represents your feelings about discussing this issue with the person who has caused the conflict in the first place. By not sorting out the conflict you not only subject yourself to a double stress-load but also lay yourself open to this person acting in the same way towards you again – after all, you never complained about it the first time!

Sometimes we do not say what we want because we feel we should not want it in the first place. If we finally express our wishes and have them granted, we are pleased but also feel a little guilty for having inconvenienced someone else. It is this reluctance to express our wishes that makes us mumble and beat about the bush, without stating clearly what it is we want,

Unresolved conflict is a considerable source of stress, so let us have a look at how you can deal with it in a constructive way.

SAYING 'NO' WITHOUT FEELING GUILTY

Imagine the following situation. You have had a gruelling week at work and you feel very tired by the time Friday evening comes around. On Sunday your parents are planning to visit, and you want to show them a good time. On Saturday morning you get a phone call from a friend who asks you whether she can drop off her three-year-old twins for two to three hours so she can spend time with an old school friend who happens to be in town that day. – What do you do?

You now have three options. You can say 'yes', you can say 'no', or you can negotiate a compromise. Your decision will depend not only on the quality of the relationship between you and your friend but also on your ability to look after yourself. If, for example, your friend habitually puts you on the spot by asking you last-minute favours, or if she cannot be relied upon to pick up her children at the agreed time, a 'no' would be justifiable. However, if your friend is reliable and generally considerate towards you, a qualified 'yes' may be a possibility. After explaining your own situation, you could check with your friend whether there is anyone else who could look after her children. If there is not, you may want to think of a convenient time when your friend can drop her children off at your place. You would also have to be specific about the number of hours that you would be willing to look after them and, if you are very tired, you would probably want to limit it to two rather than three hours.

On hearing about your situation, a real friend would in all

likelihood withdraw her request without any ill feelings, or would herself suggest that she try and find someone else. It is a common misconception that you will automatically make yourself unpopular if you do not oblige others when they ask a favour. A real friendship will not be damaged if you have to say 'no' occasionally. A relationship which is based on one person taking advantage of another, on the other hand, may come to an end over an unfulfilled request, but what would you lose if this so-called friend never spoke to you again?

A further misconception is that it is selfish to refuse to help out. However, saying 'no' is not synonymous with being rude or inconsiderate. It is important to say 'no' when you do not want to do something. It is no good saying 'yes' when you really feel 'no'. You are not doing anyone a favour and you are just creating stress for yourself by being disrespectful towards your own needs and feelings. You also create a situation where you feel resentful towards the other person, who would probably have been very understanding if only you had been honest about why you could not help out.

Think about the last time someone said 'no' to one of your requests. Provided it was done in a pleasant way, you were probably able to understand his or her reasoning and feel OK about it. If, however, you felt resentful towards this person for not consenting to your request, this might indicate that you need to do some work on the issue!

Here is a useful exercise for training yourself to say 'no' – and, as a corollary, learning to accept other people's 'no'.

THE 'NO' EXERCISE

– Make sure you are on your own in your home, unless you have a very understanding family!

– Kneel in front of your bed or sofa and hit it with your fist while shouting 'No!' Your voice should become firmer each time you shout 'no'. Continue until you feel a sense of relief. This will tell you that you have done this exercise properly.

You are likely to feel quite strange doing this exercise at first, but the fact that it feels unnatural shows that you need to do it! It is all well and good to *feel* a 'no' inside, but it will not help you with your stress unless you actually *say* it. The 'no' exercise helps you let off steam, releasing resentment and aggression and at the same time helping you voice your 'no'. That way you can say 'no' in a much nicer way next time you need to say it, because you have safely released the pressure beforehand.

SAYING WHAT YOU WANT

For babies it is straightforward to indicate what they want. All they need do is point a chubby little finger at an object and burble, and people will fall all over themselves to fetch the required item. As time goes by, however, our demands are curbed more and more. First we are taught to say 'please' and 'thank you' in connection with our request; later we learn that we cannot have everything we want. If we are *never* allowed anything we want or if we are made to feel guilty whenever we receive something we have asked for, we begin to associate negative feelings with the act of fulfilling our needs, and we may consequently come to prefer to repress them.

This will lead to problems, though, be it with family or at work. Needs do not go away just because we do not voice them. Instead, they simmer away inside, making us unhappy, anxious or resentful.

A manifestation of this process is to be found in some people (mainly women) who act as if it were their family's duty to read their mind. Unless people around them can guess accurately what they want, they withdraw and sulk or indulge themselves in moodiness. Many families are kept tiptoeing around whenever mother does not look too happy, trying all sorts of things to appease her just so the atmosphere becomes bearable again.

This is not a particularly fair way of dealing with your nearest and dearest. By leaving others to guess what you want and punishing them when they do not get it right, you are behaving like a spoiled brat. You are withholding the chance for them to get things right, at the same time feeding your own belief that no one really cares about you ('... because if they did, they would know what I want!').

Learn to say what you want. It does not devalue the result just because you asked for it. On the contrary – the more you speak about what you expect of others, the clearer a picture they get of your likes and dislikes, and the more often you will indeed get what you need and want.

Once you have said what you want and you have received what you asked for, make sure you show your appreciation. We all depend on other people's co-operation to make life pleasant, and being polite, honest and friendly will considerably smooth the way.

Things become more difficult when you are not clear about what you want. One of my clients (I will call her Angela) told me in her first session about how her husband did not understand her, how he was inconsiderate towards her and did not respect her feelings, how he only ever did what he wanted but never what she wanted. Angela was obviously distressed and felt very much on her own in her marriage. When I asked her what she actually wanted her husband to do, she could not really say. She said she did not know; all she wanted was to feel happier. – After closer inspection it turned out that Angela would have been more content if her husband spent a couple of evenings with her at home and also shared some of the housework, as they were both working. It took a long time for Angela to admit that these were the things that would improve her relationship with her husband, and even then she did not feel she was entitled to ask for them.

After we had worked through the origins of Angela's reluctance to voice her wishes and needs, she felt confident enough to express them to her husband. To her surprise he readily acquiesced and even apologized for not having helped more with the chores!

BUILDING CONFIDENCE

- Stop someone in the street and ask for the time (do not forget to take off your wrist watch beforehand), or ask for directions to a well-known place.

- Do this twice a day.

If your problem has been that you find it difficult to accept help, train your ability to do so with the following exercise.

BUILDING TRUST

- Ask friends and family to help you with small tasks, for example closing the clasp of a bracelet around your wrist, assisting you while you are preparing dinner or explaining to you something you do not understand.

Knowing what you want is especially important if you need to take a faulty item back to a shop. If you have just bought a mixer that is not working properly, the matter is fairly straightforward – you want a refund or a replacement. As you enter the shop, it is useful to bear in mind the following points:

• You do not have to prepare yourself for a fight. This is only a simple transaction, the exchange of a damaged article for either a refund or one that is in working order.

- The shop assistant dealing with your request has not personally manufactured the mixer – he or she only sells them. You are therefore not embarrassing him or her by your request.

- Your request is of a factual rather than a personal nature. You are not inconveniencing anyone or making unreasonable demands.

- All you have to say is, 'This mixer is faulty. I would like a new one or my money back, please.' Even if your self-confidence is very shaky, you will be able to say these two sentences.

For the very anxious – prepare your case.

- Do a few 'dry runs' at home in front of the mirror. Hold the mixer while you look yourself straight in the eye and say firmly to yourself in the mirror, 'This mixer is faulty. I would like a replacement or my money back, please.'

- Make sure you say it out loud, and repeat it until the words come out naturally and confidently.

Remember – if you do not speak about what is bothering you, the unreleased pressure builds up inside and puts you under stress. Better to speak about it than to choke on it!

ADDRESSING PROBLEMS

A husband who regularly works long hours notices that, over several months now, his wife has been unhappy. She is disgruntled, discontented, short with him and restless. Initially he puts this down to a prolonged spell of pre-menstrual tension, but when it continues over several weeks he discards this theory and just assumes that his wife is a difficult person. After all, he is working day and night to provide her with a comfortable lifestyle. He decides that, so long as he is patient, it will all blow over and she will become reasonable again. Anyway, she would never leave him. With a temper like hers, who else would marry her?

Eighteen months later his wife has divorced him and remarried. Her now ex-husband is working even longer hours to avoid coming home to an empty house.

Sometimes we do not want to find out what is wrong when we notice that a person has changed. A child suddenly withdraws, a husband becomes taciturn, a good friend seems suddenly to have lost her sense of humour. Whereas friends tend to pour out their hearts to each other fairly readily, family members do not always do so, for various reasons. The person who has the problem might feel embarrassed to speak about his or her worries, or perhaps he or she fears being misunderstood. When those in a work environment change and become unreliable or moody, they may feel it would be unprofessional to reveal to their colleagues what is troubling them, especially when the office atmosphere is not conducive to private talk anyway.

When people are stressed or distressed, they automatically have an effect on the people around them. People under stress are not easy to overlook, and yet we sometimes pretend that we do not see their distress for fear of what we might find out if we asked. We are afraid that we might get drawn into a complicated situation which will take up a lot of our time and which we may find we can do nothing to alleviate anyway. We might turn away from others' distress because we feel stressed ourselves and cannot face shouldering other people's woes on top of our own. Perhaps our conscience is not totally clear and we fear that we might have to listen to accusations about something we have done wrong, or that we might in fact be the cause of someone else's grief.

As long as there is a remote chance that an enquiry could spark off conflict for ourselves, we steer clear and prefer to put up with an atmosphere rather than risk unpleasant or inconvenient revelations.

The problem with sticking your head in the sand is that unresolved matters have a tendency to blow up in your face, and the resulting mess is much more difficult to tidy up than addressing the root cause in the first place.

If you ignore a problem, you relinquish control over what will happen next. Finding out why a person has changed may reveal a number of unpleasant facts, *but at least you will know what is going on.* In many cases you will discover that you have nothing to do with the other person's distress, but even if you have done something wrong it is better to know about it because it offers you the opportunity to put things right.

For the other person, discussing the problem can be a great release, even though initially he or she might find it difficult to talk about it. A distressed person will also quickly pick up whether the inquirer *really* wants to know about the problem. It is therefore helpful if you ignore the person's initial reply ('Nothing's the matter; I'm fine!') and sit down and ask again, giving feedback, for example, 'You don't look fine to me. You seem really upset. What has happened?'

There is not really an exercise I can give you to help you develop your ability to address problems more readily. Just be aware that ignoring a difficult issue does nothing to solve it; far better to sort it out as soon as possible.

ACCENTUATE THE POSITIVE

I f you spend a lot of time thinking about something, it takes on its own reality. Persistent worrying about an upcoming exam, for example, will make you physically tense and diminish your ability to concentrate, so that consequently you will do less well than if you had not got so worked up about it. Going over and over in your mind how you made a mistake at work yesterday has similar effects – you get yourself into a bad mood, you become tense and are more likely to make mistakes again the next day.

Normally we are not aware of what we are thinking throughout the day; we tend not to listen to our thoughts while we are thinking them. However, we are aware of how we *feel* and *react* as a result of our thoughts. Try it out for yourself.

TEST 1

Sit down for a moment and close your eyes. Concentrate your thoughts on a person or a situation that you dislike or fear.

– How does your body react? What changes can you perceive? How does your heart rate, your breathing, your throat and your stomach react? What is happening to the corners of your mouth?

Let at least five minutes elapse before you try out the next test.

TEST 2

Sit down and close your eyes. Now think about a person whom you like a lot, or an enjoyable event such as a recent holiday.

- How does your body react now? What are the physical signs that tell you that you are thinking about something pleasant?

Provided you use good strong examples of negative and positive persons or events, you should be able to distinguish clearly between your different physical reactions to your thoughts. Thinking about something unpleasant usually results in accelerated heartbeat, anxious breathing and general physical tension – you hunch your shoulders, clench your jaw and grit your teeth. You may also find that your fists are clenched.

As you have already seen in your mental holiday exercise (*page 72*), dwelling on pleasant and relaxing thoughts and images has exactly the opposite effect – muscles relax, the mind unwinds, and this brings with it a sense of peace and well-being.

It is important to pay attention to the quality of your thoughts because they determine how you feel during the day, how well you perform and how well you sleep at night. If you do not get rid of negative thoughts straight away, they can easily begin to fester and grow out of all proportion. You can virtually think yourself into stress.

ACQUIRING A POSITIVE OUTLOOK

So how do you get from negative to positive? Is it all a matter of putting on rose-tinted spectacles and *pretending* everything is fine when, in reality, it is not? No. Positive thinking and an optimistic outlook have nothing to do with walking around with your head in the clouds. Rather, you must work at 'shifting the balance'.

Some people, when caught up in fear of a particular situation such as their heavy workload, panic at the slightest sign of additional work coming their way. In extreme cases people can even panic at the mere *prospect* of extra work. Even though nobody has actually asked them to do more yet, they are already *thinking of what it will be like when someone finally does*. These thoughts and images may take the form of worrying about how they will cope, how they will be reprimanded if they do not perform well, and so on. The overload has not occurred, but they are already in physical and emotional overdrive.

This projection of future disaster is not just unrealistic but also a great waste of time. The disasters we fantasize about hardly ever happen, and when something goes terribly wrong it usually does so in a way that is quite unexpected. There is a superstitious belief that, unless we prepare ourselves for the worst, the worst will happen. When all goes well, we conclude that it has only done so because we worried about it first. So next time we face a difficult situation, we worry and fret some more because it worked so well last time! Worrying becomes a talisman and a habit, making us miserable for great stretches of time.

Would it not be nicer to have a good time before a major event, do well and have a good time afterwards as well? The happier you are and the more relaxed when approaching any situation in life, the better you will master the situation. This does not mean you can do without adequate preparation, though! If you want to pass your driving test, you will have to practise, practise, practise. No amount of positive thinking can help you do a three-point turn unless you have practised it first.

PRINCIPLES OF STRESS MANAGEMENT

104 What positive thinking *can* do is to get you into the right frame of mind to demonstrate your skills to their best advantage while you stay calm and focused. This relaxed attitude is also ideal should anything unexpected happen. When you are relaxed you are more likely to deal with problems constructively. So if you have had a firm belief up until now that every silver lining has a cloud, you can significantly reduce your stress levels by acquiring a positive outlook.

LIKING YOURSELF

A fundamental prerequisite for viewing the world positively is to feel good about yourself. This doesn't mean you have to consider yourself perfect, but you should at least look upon yourself as good and acceptable. Check how you feel about yourself with the following test.

TEST 3

Sit down, make yourself comfortable and think about yourself.

– What is your immediate emotional reaction? Do you feel comfortable or uncomfortable thinking about yourself?

If you feel calm and relaxed while thinking about yourself, go on to page 105. If thinking in this way makes you feel unsettled because you immediately focus on all your shortcomings, then take some time to do the following exercise.

SHIFTING THE FOCUS

Take a sheet of paper and write down everything you like about yourself. Do not stop until you have put *at least* three things down; the more the better.

If you find this exercise difficult, think about it from a slightly different angle. How would good friends of yours describe your positive qualities? Would they perhaps point out that you are a good listener or reliable or fun to be with? Or would they emphasize your helpfulness or friendliness or ability to unravel difficult situations?

Once you have written several of your good points down, sit back and consider how you would feel if you were introduced to someone at a party who had all these positive character traits. Chances are that you would like that person, wouldn't you? You would consider him or her a nice person and would feel comfortable in his or her presence ... So if *you* have these positive characteristics, you cannot be as bad as you might sometimes feel you are!

Carry your piece of paper with you for a week and look at it once a day to remind you that you are a good and worthwhile person. Spend time dwelling on your accomplishments rather than on your shortcomings for a change. Do this first thing in the morning to get the day off to a good start.

Once you feel more comfortable about yourself, it is time to tackle the issues that cause you stress.

USING AFFIRMATIONS

An affirmation is a positive phrase that you use repeatedly to feel more optimistic and to put yourself into a frame of mind that allows you to work, act and think more efficiently. The frequent use of affirmations impresses a new and more optimistic 'memory trace' onto your subconscious mind, so that after some practice you find yourself thinking more positively automatically. The most famous affirmation was developed by Emile Coué, a French psychotherapist who instructed his patients to repeat the phrase 'Every day, in every way, I am getting better and better.'

Affirmations are general statements that are designed to have an encouraging and uplifting effect, so they need to be phrased carefully. Constructing an affirmation is not difficult, provided you keep to a few basic rules.

AVOID NEGATIVE PHRASING

If possible, your affirmation should only contain positive words. Words which have to do with fear, doubt or failure should be avoided in order to get the full benefit of the affirmation. Instead of thinking 'I am not afraid of public speaking,' think, 'I am confident/calm/relaxed when I speak in public.' Instead of 'I will not make any mistakes in my exam,' think, 'I am doing well in my exam.'

USE THE PRESENT TENSE

If at all possible, avoid using future tense such as 'I *will* do well when I speak to my boss tomorrow.' Instead, say to yourself 'I am calm and relaxed when I speak to my boss.' Your subconscious mind takes things literally, so if you talk of something occurring in the future, your subconscious mind will wait and wait – but you want to feel calm *now*, so that you can approach the event with confidence and perform well when it actually takes place.

USE AFFIRMATIONS REGULARLY

Negative thoughts are usually well established by the time you get around to changing them to positive ones. This means that you might initially notice how the negative thoughts keep coming back into your mind when you are 'not looking'. Old habits die hard, and you will have to persist in replacing negative for positive every time you catch yourself. Be patient; the negative thoughts will become less powerful and will eventually vanish.

You may think that all this sounds very good and that you will definitely start with positive affirmations tomorrow. Why tomorrow? What is wrong with today? A positive thing to do is to stop procrastinating and get started right now!

POSITIVE AFFIRMATIONS FOR THE START OF THE DAY

I look forward to a happy day.
  I look forward to all the good things that are just around the corner.
  I have everything it takes to make this a good day.
  I look forward to this new day with confidence.

POSITIVE AFFIRMATIONS WHEN YOU ARE IN A DIFFICULT SITUATION

I can do this; I can solve this.
  I am calm, centred and strong.
  As I master this experience, I am getting stronger.
  I am doing my best, and my best is very good indeed.

LOOKING AT PROBLEMS AS CHALLENGES

Stress occurs when we look at any given situation as a threat rather than a challenge. When changes disrupt the smooth progression of our plans, we get angry and frustrated and act as if this hiccup jeopardizes our entire project. In reality, a disruptive event will mostly only cause a delay, and this delay can often be made up for later on. Yet our reaction to disruptive events and people is often such that we waste valuable energy being angry or anxious, spending sleepless nights and uptight days anticipating more threats to our plans.

Any problem is only as important as you make it. Most problems are minor ones; very few are genuinely devastating. Your attitude towards the problem will decide how well you deal with it. Problems are not created by a supernatural power to punish or annoy you; problems are not your enemy. Problems are essentially neutral events that you imbue with meaning, be it negative or positive.

MYTH NO. 1 – PROBLEMS CAUSE CHAOS

Unless there is some kind of genuine physical emergency at hand, problems do not have to cause havoc. The greatest chaos is likely to happen in your head, but these are only thoughts gone on the rampage. By doing any of the relaxation or breathing exercises in this book you can calm yourself down so you can think clearly again.

AFFIRMATIONS

Every problem has a solution.
　I can find a solution as I calm down.
　The sooner I calm down, the sooner I find the solution.

MYTH NO. 2 – PROBLEMS CHANGE YOUR LIFE FOR THE WORSE

Not necessarily. Being made redundant can initially come as a great shock, but it can also reveal to you a new and better direction which you would never have taken if you hadn't lost your old job. If your plans to buy a new house fall through, this may seem a disaster, but it may also lead you to even better house next time.

AFFIRMATIONS

Something good is bound to come from this.
　I can deal with this change and turn it to my advantage.
　I am going to come out tops.
　Happiness is already on its way to me.

Problems may upset other people, but they do not have to upset you. Just because everyone else gets nervous, you do not have to follow suit. You can work on taking a mental step back and assessing the problem, dividing it up into manageable parts and then dealing with them one at a time until the entire problem is solved.

Solving a problem does not require emotion. Whenever you are faced with a difficult situation, ask yourself 'Would I rather be upset or would I rather solve this?' If you prefer to solve it, get your facts straight (has there possibly been a misunderstanding?), get advice if necessary, and then implement your solution.

AFFIRMATIONS

I can stay calm and relaxed while I solve this.

I prefer to look for a solution rather than dwell on the situation as it is now.

My emotions are too valuable to me to squander them on problems.

DE-STRESS YOUR LIFE

Once stress has set in it tends to have a 'ripple' effect – lots of other areas of your life become affected. Because you are under pressure from deadlines at work, you have less time for your family, you have less time to eat and you have less time to sleep. Even though you can see that this is all wrong, you feel so much in the grip of what is happening at work that you feel unable to stop yourself from skipping meals or going to bed at an unreasonable hour every night. As a result, a life filled with stress becomes a habit, even an addiction, so that you come to consider it normal to do things that are detrimental to your health and well-being. And even though the body is remarkably resistant to being in over-drive for a while, after a while it does start to react negatively to the stresses you are placing on yourself. You lose your sense of when you have had enough. When you regularly drive yourself to exhaustion through physical, mental or emotional overwork, you deplete your energy levels to a point where you are running on empty and a collapse of some sort is on the cards. To recover from such a breakdown can take months, sometimes years, so it makes sense not to let matters get out of hand in the first place.

It is peculiar how differently people react to stress – some are incapable of eating and end up looking ill and gaunt, whereas others begin to binge, often on foods they would normally avoid. In the latter case the increase in weight makes matters worse because the person now feels unattractive and self-conscious. Apart from the emotional after-effects, overeating also puts an extra burden on the heart and the circulation. Carrying around unnecessary pounds means that your body has to work harder to help you adapt to stress and keep functioning properly. People usually binge on fatty or sweet foods, and these hinder the digestive process. As digestion itself uses up energy, this adds more strain to your already overburdened system.

You may think that you are off the hook if you do not eat very much in response to stress, but this is only partly true. Even though we tend to equate a slim body with health, this is not necessarily the case. If you are not eating properly because you are stressed, you are not providing your body with enough 'fuel' to create the energy you need to cope with stress.

Most people who are under stress do eat *something*, often while working at the same time, but they are usually eating the wrong foods. Typical stress-meals are chocolate, snack bars, endless sandwiches, coffees, teas and soft drinks, sweets or hamburgers and chips – and not a vegetable or piece of fruit in sight!

There is nothing wrong with the occasional bar of chocolate, but when you are stressed you are not doing your body a favour by giving it food that has been processed to death, offering nothing by way of fibre, vitamins or minerals but instead leaving you with excessive carbohydrates which produce acids in the body through fermentation. This is true for *all* foods that contain refined sugars, including breakfast cereals, many of which consist of up to 50 per cent sugar.

The foods that turn most readily into energy are those which are left closest to their original state, such as fresh fruit and raw or only slightly cooked vegetables. If you need something sweet when you feel stressed, go for sun-dried fruit. The less energy the body needs to spend digesting food, the more energy is left to help you deal with the stressful situation.

Make time for proper eating. Do not allow stress to prevent your body from getting the fuel it needs.

DOS AND DON'TS

- Sit down when you are eating.

- Do not eat out of packets. Put anything you eat on a plate, even if it is just a couple of biscuits.

- While you eat, do not do anything else at the same time.

- Chew properly. This helps produce enzymes in the saliva which break down food. Digestion starts in the mouth!

- Do not skip breakfast. Having some food in your stomach first thing improves concentration.

Besides eating sensibly, you can also support your body by supplying it with extra vitamins and minerals. Especially useful are vitamins A, C and E, also known as antioxidants, which help combat free radicals in the body (these free radicals can destabilize healthy cells). If you are of a nervous disposition, you will find magnesium very helpful. Ideally, take it together with the same amount of calcium. Magnesium has a soothing effect on the nerves and helps you relax better.

Seventy-five per cent of the human body consists of water, and 72 per cent of our blood is made up of water. It is the water in the blood that carries nourishment to the cells and helps rid the body of toxins by flushing through the kidneys regularly. It is recommended that you drink between six and eight glasses of water each day to enable your body to function properly. This water should be filtered or bottled only; tap water, although safe to drink, has a much higher chlorine content than bottled water – the less chlorine you take into the body, the better for your health; after all, chlorine is bleach.

Tea and coffee, including decaffeinated coffee, are no substitutes for water! Caffeine dehydrates the body and hypes you up artificially by increasing your heart rate; it can cause insomnia, trembling, nervousness and muscle tension – all conditions you can do without when you are already stressed.

Alcohol may seem to help you relax, but excessive use of it causes the body to accumulate toxins and eradicates the B vitamins and vitamin C as well as minerals. Alcohol can also cause sleeping problems, impairs immune function and makes you feel depressed, thus adding to the already existing stress burden.

THINK BEFORE YOU START WORKING

When you are wound up and afraid that you may not be able to do all the work that needs doing, some people tend to rush into activity and press on throughout the day without stopping. This may look impressive to outsiders, but it is not the most intelligent way of tackling a great workload. You may think you are saving time, but in reality you are floundering without a plan so that in fact you are *wasting* time.

Any activity can be spread over a period of hours or days;

planning what you need to achieve each day is crucial. The easiest way to do so is to start the day by making a list.

- Write down everything that needs doing.

- Mark those items that are urgent.

- Now extract those items from the 'urgent' list which you do not like doing – then do them first to get them out of the way!

- Be prepared to cancel or postpone those items which are not very important if you are running out of time at the end of the day.

- Set a time limit of how late you want to work – and stick to it.

- Take breaks, especially when you feel there is absolutely no time for a break. Stopping for only two to three minutes and relaxing can make all the difference; it clears your head and helps you concentrate better.

- Make it a rule to complete one task before you start the next. You may not finish everything on your list, but at least you will have completed most items rather than having made only a half-hearted stab at all of them.

GET A MOVE ON – EXERCISE!

When you are under stress your body tenses up and various stress hormones are released into the bloodstream. When you do not move your body, for example if you spend a lot of time sitting at a desk, your limbs stay tense and the adrenalin keeps you hyped up for longer than necessary. This is why it can sometimes be difficult to unwind even after a stressful event has passed – the adrenalin still keeps your mind whizzing so that you find it impossible to relax. Even just *thinking* about a stressful situation keeps the body in a state of tension.

This is where exercise comes into it, and you will be pleased to learn that exercise in this context *does not mean hours of work-outs five times a week*. There is a great myth, no doubt brought about by the recent fitness culture, that only if you puff and pant at the end of your exercise routine will you have done your body any good. This is not so. You can achieve very good results from even just ten minutes of exercise, provided you do it regularly – that is, every other day at least. It is not necessary to get into a slinky leotard or to join an expensive health club. Working adrenalin out of your system can be fun and does not have to make you go purple in the face. Here are some simple exercise routines which you can do indoors or (weather permitting) out.

EXERCISE 1 – CYCLING

– Lie down on your back on a firm mattress or on a blanket on the floor.

– Support your head by putting a small cushion under it.

– Put your arms flat on the floor next to your body.

– Begin to make cycling movements with your legs in the air, but make sure your whole back remains on the ground.

– Count 'one' for every right-left leg movement you do; continue to the count of 60.

EXERCISE 2 – STRETCHING

– Stand with your face to a wall.

– Place both hands against the wall, keeping your arms straight.

– Pretend you are trying to push the wall away by keeping

your right leg bent, right foot flat on the floor, and the left leg stretched out straight behind the right one, left foot flat on the floor. You should feel a gentle stretch in the back of your left leg. (Should the stretch feel uncomfortable, bring your left leg nearer to the right leg.)

– Hold the stretch to the count of 60 (approximately 1 minute), then change feet so the left leg is in the forward position and the right leg behind. Feel the stretch in your right leg. Hold for 60.

– Throughout, make sure you keep your arms straight, pushing into the wall.

EXERCISE 3 – RUNNING

– Take your shoes off and stand on your bed. Alternatively, fold up an old blanket several times so it becomes really thick. Should you decide to do this exercise on the floor, make sure you wear firm shoes, ideally trainers, to cushion your joints adequately.

– Run on the spot, counting one for every right-left leg movement. Do the exercise to the count of 120.

Now go through the whole sequence of cycling, stretching and running one more time, then finish off with a last stretching exercise. All this will take you about ten minutes. It gets your muscles loose and increases your heart rate so that the adrenalin gets cleared out of your system and your head is de-fogged. Make sure you drink some water, one or two glasses, afterwards so that toxins and body wastes can be eliminated more easily.

Swimming a few lengths in a pool – just as many as you can do without feeling uncomfortable – or walking briskly for ten minutes are equally good alternatives. If you choose walking, make sure you wear firm shoes with thick soles.

Whether you are an executive of an international company or at home with several small children (the workload is approximately the same in both cases), make sure there is more to your life than the work you are doing! When you are buzzing with activities and duties day in and day out, it is easy to forget your own needs and interests in the process.

Having at least one hobby or interest that you pursue fairly regularly is a safeguard against becoming overwrought. Even if you love your job, it is therapeutic to engage in activities that have nothing to do with work. Whether you like collecting stamps or playing golf, whether you want to learn to roller-skate or fly a kite, make the time to do something special, something that is fun and just for you.

Having outside interests also helps you to take a step back from your work and put it into a more balanced perspective. By making space for outside interests in your life it becomes possible to take a more detached look at your work when you get back to it; often, solutions for work problems come to mind much more easily once you have not thought about them for a while.

Above all, having outside interests is an excellent way of recharging your batteries and gathering fresh enthusiasm, and it beats watching television any day!

ALTERNATIVE WAYS TO UNWIND

As we have discussed, there are lots of things you can do to keep stress from developing in the first place and to deal with it effectively. Ideally you will always try and deal with the underlying cause of your stress rather than with its symptoms, but that is not always possible. Sometimes all you can do is to hang on in there and deal with a difficult situation as best you can.

If you find yourself in a situation where stress symptoms have become firmly established, it can be useful to get outside assistance to help you unwind. There are a number of natural therapies which can support your own efforts and help you get relief from stress symptoms more quickly. There follow brief descriptions of some of these therapies, to give you an idea of how they can help with stress. Should you decide to pursue any of them further, you will find suggestions for further reading and some useful addresses at the end of each section.

AROMATHERAPY

Aromatherapy uses essential oils taken from plants, to be massaged into the skin, inhaled or taken orally. If the oil is to be absorbed via the skin, a good aromatherapist will very carefully clean the skin first and then help the skin absorb the oil by applying hot compresses after the oil has been applied. Another way of encouraging the oil to pass through the skin is by gently massaging it into the face or back.

Aromatherapy oils can benefit a vast range of physical, emotional and mental symptoms. Oils that help with nervous tension are bergamot, chamomile, geranium, jasmine, marjoram, rose and sandalwood.

FURTHER READING

C. Hopkins, *Principles of Aromatherapy* (Thorsons, 1996).
C. McGilvery and J. Reed, *Essential Aromatherapy* (Acropolis Books, 1993).

To find a qualified practitioner, contact:

Aromatherapy Organisations Council
3 Latymer Close
Braybrooke
Market Harborough
Leics LE16 8LN

HYPNOTHERAPY

Hypnosis is a combination of relaxation and concentration, and as such is very useful in combating the negative effects of stress. A few sessions of suggestion therapy, together with a good self-hypnosis tape, should be sufficient to teach you how to let go of physical tension so that your body and mind can calm down and recharge.

The relaxing effect of hypnosis is usually brought about by suggestions of soothing mental images which you are encouraged to concentrate on; by focusing on a pleasant and reassuring picture in your mind, you help your body to relax.

FURTHER READING

V. Peiffer, *Principles of Hypnotherapy* (Thorsons, 1996).
M. H. Erickson and E. Rossi, *Experiencing Hypnosis: Therapeutic Approaches to Altered States* (Irvington, 1981).

To find a qualified practitioner, contact:

The Corporation of Advanced Hypnotherapy
PO Box 70
Southport
Merseyside PR8 3JB

REFLEXOLOGY

Reflexology is guided by the principle that various pressure points on the feet correspond to different centres of the body.

After gently feeling your feet, a reflexologist will apply pressure to various points where a 'block' has been detected under the skin. These blocks indicate that the internal organ which corresponds to that particular pressure point is not functioning to its full capacity. By pressing a particular point, the organ is stimulated. Reflexology has achieved good results in treating, among other conditions, stress states, headaches and constipation.

FURTHER READING

N. Hall, *Principles of Reflexology* (Thorsons, 1996).
E. D. Ingham, *Stories the Feet Can Tell Thru Reflexology* (New York: Ingham Publishing, 1984).

To find a qualified practitioner, contact:

Monks Orchard
Whitbourne
Worcester WR6 5RB

International Council for Reflexology
4311 Stockton Boulevard
Sacramento
CA 95820
USA

SHIATSU

Shiatsu massage works with the acupuncture points situated along energy paths in the body (also know as meridians). Depending on which meridians are stimulated, the practitioner can help the client feel toned up or calmed down. Shiatsu is used both prophylactically and for specific conditions.

Pressure is applied with the fingers, and sometimes also with the palms or elbows while the client lies on a padded mat. Shiatsu is also useful as a self-help technique (Do-In).

FURTHER READING

C. Jarmey, *Principles of Shiatsu* (Thorsons, 1996).
E. Shaw, *60-Second Shiatzu* (Simon and Schuster, 1990).

To find a qualified practitioner, contact:

The Shiatsu Society
19 Langside Park
Kilbarchan
Renfrewshire PA10 2EP

Positive thinking counsellors teach you how to access the sub-conscious level of your mind and how to implant positive suggestions and affirmations there. They also help you uncover any unhelpful beliefs and attitudes you may have so you can change them to more positive and constructive ones.

The methods used are easy to learn and very effective at reducing physical tension and anxiety, and helping you to boost your self-confidence.

FURTHER READING

V. Peiffer, *Positive Thinking* (Element Books, 1989).
N. V. Peale, *The Power of Positive Thinking* (Cedar, 1953).

To find a qualified practitioner, contact:

The Peiffer Foundation
PO Box 2517
London W5 5LN

SUMMARY

onstant stress is not only unpleasant, it is also bad for
your health. You may be tempted to ignore your stress
symptoms because it is easier to carry on as usual than
to stop and think about ways to alleviate your stress, but this is
at best only a short-term solution. The reasons why many people are reluctant to deal with their stress are that they do not
know where to start or how to go about it, as well as being worried that dealing with their stress might mean changing their
lifestyle completely.

Hopefully this book will have shown you ways to combat
stress that suit you so that your questions of where to start and
how to go on are solved. As to fears about dramatic changes in
your life, let me reassure you that in most cases the only thing
you need to change is your attitude. This is not necessarily easy,
but it is worth doing as it can make a great difference to your
future well-being and success in life.

On those occasions where you do have to make a big change,
such as separating from a partner or leaving an unsuitable job,
you are better off doing so before you are so stressed out that
you haven't the energy to take positive action.

Remember, you are worth looking after – please do so!

INDEX

By the same author

PRINCIPLES OF HYPNOTHERAPY

VERA PEIFFER

Interest in hypnotherapy has grown rapidly over the last few years. Many people are realizing that it is an effective way to solve problems such as mental and emotional trauma, anxiety, depression, phobias and confidence problems, and eliminate unwanted habits such as smoking. This introductory guide explains:

- what hypnotherapy is

- how it works

- what its origins are

- what to expect when you go for treatment

- how to find a reputable hypnotherapist

Vera Peiffer is a leading authority on hypnotherapy. She is a psychologist in private practice in West London specializing in analytical hypnotherapy and a member of the Corporation of Advanced Hypnotherapy.

ENERGIZE YOURSELF

A COMPLETE GUIDE TO RESTORING
LOST VITALITY AND STRENGTH

VERA PEIFFER

This practical handbook not only looks at the causes of depleted energy, but also suggests ways in which you can recharge your physical and emotional batteries. Vera Peiffer introduces many down-to-earth methods and techniques aimed at achieving this, all of which are highly effective and fun to carry out.

Discover the benefits of vitamins and minerals, detoxifying, rebounding, breathing, stretching, relaxing, meditating, creative visualization, enjoying music, homoeopathy, shiatsu and much, much more.

Ideal for anyone who feels lethargic, listless or who has recently been ill, *Energize Yourself* is essential reading for anyone needing a kick start in life.

STRESS

PROVEN STRESS-COPING STRATEGIES FOR BETTER HEALTH

LEON CHAITOW

Do you suffer from migraine, chronic back pain, frequent colds, fatigue, panic attacks or high blood pressure? If so, too much stress could be damaging your health.

Stress has a disastrous effect on our immune systems, and can be the major cause of both mild and serious health problems. Psychoneuroimmunology, or PNI, is the science which holds the key to many common health problems. It points to new ways to control these damaging emotions and so protect our bodies' natural defences and ward off illness.

Leading health writer Leon Chaitow here uses the latest research into the mind/body connection to help you create your own stress protection plan. Advice on diet, exercise, meditation, relaxation, guided imagery and visualization, with useful checklists, will help you develop your own system to cope with the inevitable pressures of life.

Leon Chaitow, osteopath, naturopath and acupuncturist, is a leading international practitioner and successful author of a wide range of health books.

PRINCIPLES OF HYPNOTHERAPY	0 7225 3242 3	£4.99	☐
ENERGIZE YOURSELF!	0 7225 3111 7	£6.99	☐
STRESS	0 7225 3192 3	£5.99	☐

All these books are available from your local bookseller or can be ordered direct from the publishers.

To order direct just tick the titles you want and fill in the form below:

Name: _____

Address: _____

_____

_____ Postcode: _____

Send to: Thorsons Mail Order, Dept 3, HarperCollins*Publishers*, Westerhill Road, Bishopbriggs, Glasgow G64 2QT.
Please enclose a cheque or postal order or your authority to debit your Visa/Access account –

Credit card no: _____

Expiry date: _____

Signature: _____

– to the value of the cover price plus:
UK & BFPO: Add £1.00 for the first book and 25p for each additional book ordered.
Overseas orders including Eire: Please add £2.95 service charge. Books will be sent by surface mail but quotes for airmail despatches will be given on request.

24 HOUR TELEPHONE ORDERING SERVICE FOR ACCESS/VISA CARDHOLDERS – TEL: 0141 772 2281.